TOUGH QUESTIONS

TOUGH QUESTIONS ABOUT HEALING

Derek Frank

Highland Books
Guildford, Surrey

Published by Highland Books, an imprint of Inter Publishing Service
(IPS) Ltd, 59 Woodbridge Road, Guildford, Surrey GU1 4RF.

All scripture quotations, unless otherwise noted, are taken from the
Holy Bible, New International Version Copyright 1973, 1978, 1984 by the
International Bible Society.
Used by permission of Hodder & Stoughton.

Typeset by Electronic Book Factory Ltd, Fife, Scotland.
Printed in the UK by HarperCollins Manufacturing, Glasgow.

ISBN No: 0 897913 01 X

CONTENTS

ACKNOWLEDGEMENTS

Though the writing of this book came about through my personal journey, that journey was only sustainable because of the help and support I received from many different people.

I would first like to acknowledge the Revd Canon Robert Warren, not only for his Foreword written as National Officer for the Decade of Evangelism, but for the privilege of the six years I spent on the staff of St Thomas, Crookes in Sheffield when he was Rector. Such ability as I have to reflect on my experience of the ministry of healing is largely due to the stimulus of his thinking. I also want to thank another former member of the staff of St Thomas: Revd Dr Mark Stibbe, for his timely and expert help in reshaping the manuscript.

The loving support of the 9.15 congregation and others within St Thomas, both prayerfully and practically, played a crucial role in upholding me, especially in the tougher moments. I also want to particularly acknowledge my wife, Françoise, and my daughters, Vanessa and Abigail, for the unfailing constancy of their love, not just through a season of illness, but then through a season of writing!

By far the most important acknowledgement is however of what the Lord has done, both in restoring my health, and in enabling me to explore some tough questions on the way. I trust that as you think with me about them, you will not conclude that I would have done better to 'avoid foolish questions ... for they are unprofitable' (Titus 3:9 A.V.) Instead that you may have something of the experience of the Queen of Sheba! Her willingness to travel a journey in order to work through some hard questions (1 Kings 10:1) resulted in more than just having all her questions answered. It caused her to exclaim 'Praise be to the Lord' (v9).

My prayer is that as we honestly face the questions that do exist about the healing ministry, that far from being discouraged, we may see yet greater reason to glorify the Lord our God.

FOREWORD

There are many reasons why I am glad to commend this book. Not least is the fact that the author, Derek Frank, and I worked together on the same staff team for six years. As the leader of that team I valued his sharp and purposeful contributions. His eagerness for the church to discover and do the will of God did not always make for a quiet life, but it certainly enriched the work we were involved in. Significantly his contribution was often in searching out the real issues and fearlessly addressing them. In other words, he was always asking the 'tough questions'.

But the greatest 'tough questions' he was involved in during this period were the ones that life asked of him when he found himself both committed to the conviction that God heals today, and at the same time faced with a potentially life-threatening illness. This book is the story of Derek's wrestling with those questions.

However, it is more than a story. It is the thoughtful reflection on some tough questions which need facing today: questions not faced in a peaceful academic setting, but in the dark wilderness night when God seems to go quiet, and in the heart of the crucible of mixed and distressing emotions about an unknown or feared future.

A further reason for wanting to commend this book is that I saw it being written. Not physically, but yet truly. I did not see Derek put pen to paper, or rather finger to keyboard, but I did catch glimpses of a divine hand etching change and growth on the parchment of

Derek's character and experience of life. For this book is the story of one person's – sometimes painful and necessarily solitary – journey not only into healing, but also into personal growth and maturing of vision of the greatness of God's purposes for the whole of creation.

The actual writing of the book was almost accidental. It was really a form of 'journalling' which Derek did whilst recovering from illness. Or rather, because it did not start out as a book, it was a form of occupational therapy for a person too weak to get up off a chair, but too restless just to sit. It was only later that the thought of publication emerged.

After an energetic first six years in the ordained ministry Derek found himself laid out with no energy to do anything. It was, humanly speaking, a sickness least sympathetic to his temperament. Yet, as the book bears eloquent testimony, it was an act of God, defined not as a disaster of massive proportions, but rather as the opening of a door into a whole new way of seeing God, himself, life and human society.

The book is an interweaving of respect for Scripture as God's revelation to us, honesty about his own experience, courage to face tough questions, a willingness to grow and change as a person, and a determination to come out believing – even if the nature of the believing, and character of the one believing, is matured greatly.

A further reason for wanting to commend this book is that it addresses issues that have been crying out for attention.

The healing ministry in the church is all too easily divided into two camps. The 'faith camp' feels asking tough questions is evidence of unbelief; the 'tough questions' camp ends up doubting whether any healing actually takes place. This book wrestles, from a position of faith, with those tough questions. The result is a reshaping of faith and a maturing of understanding about wider issues. Those issues include such matters as what Scripture means by the healing of the nations, the place of Job in the healing vision, and the healing of the whole creation, These are matters not usually addressed in what are called 'healing circles'.

My other reason for commending this book is that it shows us someone 'doing theology'. Theology is not something we often think of 'doing'. We expect people to study or teach it. But 'doing theology' is taking the raw material of life, bringing it before the plumb-line of Scripture, and seeking to discern the mind and will of God in the interaction between the Word and life, between 'theory and practice'. One of the surest signs of having done a good job about this practice of theology is that we are changed in the process. Jacob wrestling with the angel is the model of someone 'doing theology'. The real test of how well such work is done is not to be found in what truth we get hold of so much as in how the truth gets hold of us in the very process of our wrestling with it. From that perspective this is a good piece of doing theology.

For all these reasons I commend this book. It is full of insights quarried from the deep seams of adversity and lack of hope. It come out of a real personal pilgrimage through illness, a determination to trust God's Word and find answers to tough questions, and a willingness to change, learn, grow and be shaped by our experience of life. That has relevance well beyond the issues of this book. It even shows the way to those who may feel some of the answers do not satisfy: how to wrestle with our unanswered questions in the way that the author shows us.

To do that would indeed enrich the life of the whole church, as well of any individual so committed.

Robert Warren

1

Is This All There Is To Healing?

It was with both disbelief and anxiety that I viewed the X-ray of my chest hanging on the wall behind the consultant. I'd been told that cloudiness was one of the signs of sarcoidosis, a rare disease which my father had died of when he was my age.

Even my medically-untrained eye could see a big white patch on the X-ray, and the consultant seemed to be taking an eternity to come to the point. My impatience got the better of me.

'Doctor – I can see that there's a large white patch over one of my lungs,' I interjected.

Unfortunately, my attempt at sounding confident was thrown by his laughter.

'So you should,' he replied 'that's your heart!'

Relief! That is until he continued. 'No, what you need to see is this.'

Then he put on the light behind the X-ray and showed me the distinctive pattern it revealed.

'Of course we can't be sure until you've had the Kveim test, and that'll take another eight weeks I'm sorry to say . . .'

Quite what he went on to say to me thereafter I really can't remember. I'm sure he must have explained that sarcoidosis can burn itself out and that steroids can be very helpful in controlling its effects. My mind however could only think of the way I had been taken over by increasing tiredness in recent months. For some time I'd been feeling as if I were at the top of a slippery slope, and that rather like the Cresta run, once you've started, there's no stopping the journey before you cross the finishing line. Except in this case there were no medals to be won for making it down in the fastest possible time.

I'd spent the first ten impressionable years of my life watching my father progressively die of sarcoidosis, and here I was facing the same diagnosis. I thought of my young family, of my congregation at church, of the vision of ministry that God had given me. The question was, what could I do to slow the journey down that slippery slope?

Looking back, I find it shocking to see how shallow my faith was at that point, despite all I have sought to teach about faith for healing. The fact was that in God's providence, and also in an open-air jacuzzi in Los Angeles (but that's another story!) I had already met someone God had dramatically healed of sarcoidosis. Yet even this carried no weight. God had indeed gone ahead to prepare the way even before I knew what was wrong with me. However, at that stage I had little perception of His hand in what was going on.

I had also heard the testimony of Peter Jennings, healed of sarcoidosis when John Wimber discerned an afflicting spirit that lay behind his condition. The *Renewal* magazine article from some years earlier describing Peter's virtually instantaneous healing was still on my shelves.[1] Entitled 'Cured of a killer disease', it told of how a severe form of the disease had begun to take over his whole body, from his ankles and legs, to his vision. Not only was his right eye 90 per cent blind, but tests showed that his kidneys and liver were also affected. The consultant had told him that no one knew how or why it came, and as yet, no one had discovered a cure.

In his capacity as European correspondent for *Our Sunday Visitor*, the largest-selling Roman Catholic weekly newspaper in the USA, Peter had sought an interview with John Wimber when he was at the Acts '86 conference in Birmingham. They had met briefly in the lobby of John's hotel to arrange a time for an interview. It was only in passing that Peter mentioned his illness. John and his wife Carol left Peter to take the lift. However, despite John's protestations about a somewhat urgent need to locate the bathroom, Carol felt a conviction that they should go back to pray for him. The compromise solution was a high-speed return to find Peter, and a relatively brief time of prayer! After only a few moments of prayer on the pavement outside the Metropole Hotel, John said to Peter 'I believe that in the power of Jesus, we can break the spirit of this disease in your body.' Following a few more moments of prayer he smiled saying 'You're OK now; God is telling me that the disease is no longer in your body. Go and see your doctors and see what they say.'

Then with characteristic humour, he added 'That'll be one and ninepence please,' but before Peter could reply John and Carol had set off. Ten minutes had been a very short time for the miracle of healing which had taken place in Peter, yet apparently no one else appreciated just how long it had been for John! Within one hour the vision had returned to Peter's right eye, and within three hours the vitality which he had so acutely lacked for months suddenly returned. He later described how his amazing recovery left him feeling like Superman, wanting to go round picking up mountains.

Regular and extensive hospital tests confirmed that, though there was no medical explanation of what had happened. As a religious journalist who had always exercised great caution in writing about healing, Peter sought the co-operation of the doctors involved in investigating his remarkable recovery. There was no other explanation. It was God who had healed him of sarcoidosis in a miraculous way.

Whatever the miracle Peter was privileged to have received, the fact was that those who prayed for me were unable to minister a similarly immediate one. I thought the member of our church who suggested flying me over to John Wimber to be prayed for by him was

joking. Far from it, he meant it. The reason I declined
was not through reluctance in receiving such generosity.
It was for another reason entirely. I had already come to
the conclusion that the way God heals is unpredictable.
God had special purposes in touching Peter Jennings in
the way He had, which were not just to do with John
Wimber's predicament at that moment in time. Neither
was it that God loved me any less than Peter. However,
I sensed that what God wanted to do in and through me,
would not be achieved by a made-to-measure miracle,
desirable as one would have been.

However, though a miracle did not seem to be on offer,
something else did seem to be. It appeared to be an
invitation to grapple with what the healing ministry is
about. Where has it come from? Why has it reached where
it has? What is it heading towards? I felt God was inviting
me to engage with these issues, not from the position of
a dispassionate commentator, but from the standpoint
of one with a vested interest. The invitation was to face
the tough questions that arise when healing doesn't come
to order. I felt neither physically or theologically up to
the invitation, nor did I particularly want it. Yet, as I
reflected on where the healing ministry seems to have
reached, I realized that not many of those who are
physically and theologically up to it are responding to
it. Not a little reluctantly, I accepted the invitation.

Taking stock of the healing ministry

I began reflecting on the tough questions that we now
have about the healing ministry that we didn't have ten
or twenty years ago, when there was less expectancy for
healing. Could it be, I wondered, that we have reached
the upper limit in the ministry of healing, and this is all
there is to it? Is this the pinnacle of what is possible this
side of eternity? In the light of John 14:12 it seemed a
little unlikely! Jesus' promise was that 'anyone who has
faith in me will do what I have been doing. He will do

even greater things than these, because I am going to the Father'.

Even the most ardent enthusiast for the healing ministry would scarcely describe what we have at the moment in these terms. The tough questions we face must surely be pointing to something else, even though it may require much reflection to understand what that might be.

I soon found myself considering what the consequences will be if the church just settles for its present experience of healing, simply sweeping the tough questions under the carpet. In the short-term it will presumably be possible to continue doing just that. We've been doing it for a while already, and can probably do it a while longer yet. How long will it be before what's been swept under the carpet causes bumps which the church will trip over, maybe even falling flat on its face? In the Decade of Evangelism, what view will the world take of a church that proclaims healing, but which looks increasingly stuck in the practical doing of what it proclaims?

On the other hand, what opportunity lies in seeing these questions as God's way of leading the church into a far deeper understanding of His purposes in healing? Perhaps there's some relevance in the picture of a schoolmaster who stretches his pupils' understanding by asking questions which are always just one step ahead of where they've reached? Could it be in this Decade of Evangelism, which ultimately is focused on the healing of the relationship with God of a fallen world, that He is wanting to communicate a more profound understanding of healing than that which we currently have? One which might impact the lives of many who presently see little relevance in the message of the church?

The more I reflected on this, the more I realized that there is urgent need to take stock of where the healing ministry has reached. Despite the tough questions about apparently unanswered prayers for healing, these are still remarkable times that we live in. It's been said that 'when all is said and done, rather more is said than done.'

This is certainly true in the ministry of healing. Yet what can be rejoiced in is that rather more is being done than ever used to be. Across the denominations, faith exists for at least a measure of healing to be ministered. Different, methodologies and theologies of healing co-exist. A sign outside one church read 'Try our healing service – you won't get better.' Yet underlying them all is the same conviction. The Holy Spirit is present to heal, and not just through a few gifted individuals, but through the body of the church. There has been a remarkable recovery of belief in the effective presence of a God who acts.

At the same time, the gap between the vision for healing and the reality of it is very real. Perhaps the most prominent example of unanswered prayer for healing was the death of David Watson. He had enormous faith, and was prayed for by many who had seen prayers for healing answered very powerfully, including John Wimber. Why then was he not healed in order to be available for The Decade of Evangelism? Recently, John Wimber himself has needed medical treatment. The story of Jennifer Rees-Larcombe in *Unexpected Healing*, healed after eight years of encephalitis, having been told that there was no cure for her condition, is inspirational. Yet what is the answer to her child who said 'If God can do this now, why didn't He make you better when we were smaller and needed you more?'[2]

Alongside the tough questions raised by these and other publicised stories, are the questions arising from the countless private stories of unanswered prayer for healing. The tough questions sit there unanswered, not only for those who have been prayed for, but also for those who did the praying. Is it that God doesn't love them? Is it that they didn't have enough faith? Is it that they didn't pray the right way? Is it . . .? The questions go on.

For the chronically sick, to face being prayed for one more time, with the risk of yet another unanswered prayer, can simply be too much. For those who have prayed from the bottom of their hearts and seen no answer in situations of profound need, to sustain such ministry with vitality and faith can become more and more difficult.

As the healing ministry goes on from year to year, inevitably the residue of unanswered prayers grows. It is therefore increasingly necessary that we find the ways of handling these tough questions. Not only that we may hear what God is saying to us about how to reach out with greater effectiveness to minister healing into a broken world. It is even more fundamental than this. If we don't, what we have in the healing ministry to date could be lost, as we back off from taking risks for fear of our prayers not being answered.

Facing the questions

The consequence of a progressive retrenchment in the healing ministry could be very hard to reverse. Just as muscles which are used less and less gradually atrophy, so it could well be with faith for healing. What it would then take to persuade us to face the necessary spiritual physiotherapy to renew our atrophied faith-muscle is hard to imagine. It may seem a massive assignment to fully own and face the tough questions we have about healing, neither denying their complexities, nor losing sight of the vision. However, the consequences of not doing so may be far greater.

Furthermore, we might not have an indefinite amount of time in which to do so. In the Early Church, the momentum for healing was not quickly lost. Nonetheless, from the fourth century onwards, what had been the confirming sign for the preaching of the gospel had become only a small thread in the much bigger story of the church. Though it was never totally lost,[3] what had been such a vital part of the witness that had led to around one-fifth of the Roman empire being converted by the end of the first century, had by the fourth century become

more notional than normative. Given that the Western
church, notwithstanding the outpouring of the Holy Spirit
this century, has scarcely even begun to evangelize in the
context of signs and wonders, history suggests that not
only might the same happen to our own experience of
healing, but also that it might happen much sooner than
we realize.

Such loss puts the cost of grappling with the tough
questions into another perspective. If we're serious about
the ministry of healing, or more to the point, serious about
moving forward with God, then to sweep these questions
under the carpet is an inane thing to do. Few material
things of any worth in this world have been secured without costly perseverance: how much more should we be
willing to pay to advance the things of spiritual worth?

The history of aviation exemplifies what it costs to face
tough questions in order to secure even purely technical
development. *Those Magnificent Men in Their Flying
Machines* was made as a humorous film centred on
the first days of flying. The initial footage of early
attempts to fly, though hilarious from our perspective,
makes a serious point. The pioneers used extraordinarily
risky contraptions to prove that machines which were
heavier than air really could leave the ground. From
today's perspective their attempts seem laughable, yet
their efforts deserve our respect. Were it not for their
brave determination to persevere in the face of so much
heartache and disaster, including loss of life, we would
not be flying today let alone have Concorde or space
travel.

The big breakthrough was achieved when the first flights
took place. The ultimate question had been answered. The
law of gravity could be superseded by another law – the
law of flight. Yet it was only because of subsequent perseverance that the benefit was extended to everyone. In
the face of much cynical scepticism that it would never be
commercially viable, the pioneers pressed on, grappling
with wave upon wave of tough questions. Each one had

to be faced. Nothing could be swept under the carpet. The cost had only just begun when the first breakthrough was made, yet nowadays no one would question the rightness of those apparently crazy pioneers pressing on with what it took to get to the answers.

Compared with the ministry of healing, aviation is a very down-to-earth business! With the rediscovery that the laws of sickness can be superseded by a greater law – the law of supernatural healing, the big breakthrough has happened. Yet if in aviation the greatest perseverance was required to answer the tough questions which arose subsequent to the big breakthrough, how much more with the ministry of healing. The fact that it is not just costly, but personally painful to do so, is no reason to avoid doing what is needed.

Pray – not prey

What is involved in the development of the healing ministry poses an even greater challenge to perseverance than anything in the realm of technology. Whereas it was only aeronautical difficulties and the discouragement of the sceptics that the pioneers were up against, in the healing ministry we have an enemy who is actively out to take back off us the ground that we have just secured.

In the parable of the sower in Matthew 13, Jesus begins with a picture of the seed falling on the path. This the birds came and ate up. Jesus later interpreted what it meant. 'When anyone hears the message about the kingdom and does not understand it, the evil one comes and snatches away what is sown in his heart' (v19). Random scattering of seed may not at first sight be something we naturally relate to. However, as anyone who has sown a lawn knows, the parable speaks volumes about the need to deter the birds until after the seed is sufficiently established. This requires a good downpour of rain and some time following in order that proper root systems might develop.

So far, it cannot be said that the seed of the healing ministry is fully germinated, let alone that it has had time to develop proper root systems. The ability to pray for healing remains prey to the destroyer. It requires active protection, which is not to be found in sweeping the tough questions under the carpet, but only by fully acknowledging them and working with them. Just as the Twelve, despite all their difficulties in learning to minister healing, were made custodians of it for future generations, so in our time, despite all our difficulties with it, are we.

The new start that we are being offered in God's grace and mercy is surely not just intended as material for short-term revivalism. It is one of those rare opportunities in church history to re-lay the foundations for years to come. The tough questions may seem like rather big blocks in the way of doing this, especially when they are presently in our own lives. Despite how we may feel about God's gift of a miracle to one person and not to another, it remains with us as to whether they become stumbling blocks, or starting blocks for healing.

What follows is an attempt to articulate some of those questions, that we might consider what God may be saying to us through them about a more mature understanding of the ministry of healing.

2

Why Doesn't God Do Miracles More Often?

For a time after my diagnosis I tried to continue keeping up appearances, but life was like a colour television which most days could only manage black and white. Occasional glimmerings of colour, mostly monochrome, but sometimes even the black and white had become difficult to distinguish. Amidst it I sought to continue my reflections on the healing ministry. At the same time, I became uncomfortably aware that God might well be wanting to touch some issues in my life. However as far as I was concerned, getting physically well was the number one priority, and in the minimum time possible. I had things to get on with. All I really wanted to do was to get back to how I'd been before my illness.

Yet despite encouraging words and pictures from several people that this was not 'a sickness unto death', that it 'would leave its mark, but that I would completely recover'; and despite receiving much prayer, I only felt worse. The previous summer, wind-surfing on the Pacific with the seals eying my toes for tea, seemed a very long while ago. Regularly I wondered where God was in all this.

Increasingly I began to question why God doesn't move in the way we would expect. I had first-hand evidence that He was willing to do a miracle to more or less instantaneously remove the type of illness I had. I had first-hand evidence that He is a God of great mercy, who hears and answers prayer. Yet in this moment of great personal need He seemed to be elusive, if not absent. It

felt as if I'd been lured into playing hide and seek with the
Almighty. It was something I scarcely had the inclination
for, particularly as He had all the advantages. Yet I suspected much hinged on my willingness to participate.

As I did so, I discovered the signs of His presence
somewhere quite different from where I'd started looking.
It came about through realizing that in my conversation
with God, the wires were crossed. My prayer had been
for Him to heal me physically, and should there along
the way be any healing of my inner self, that would be
a bonus. I began to recognize that God might be wanting
first and foremost to heal me inwardly. Should there be
some physical healing, perhaps this was in His view less
of a priority, maybe even just a bonus. My prayer had
been 'God – get me back to where I was'. God was
saying 'That's the last place I want to take you: I'm
only interested in taking you somewhere new!' For God
and I to reach any agreement in what was to happen, one
of us was going to have to move position!

Somewhat reluctantly, I tried to think more about
God's perspective on my healing than my own. If there
was to be any healing in my life, it would only be by
receiving what He, the Healer, wanted to do. Maybe that
would involve letting go of some of my more dogmatic
presuppositions, which I had never really thought to
question before. Maybe, they just needed reshaping.
Perhaps in the process of this God might even start
me on the journey towards the more mature model of
the healing ministry I was seeking.

I began to reflect on my reasons for seeing God's highest
and best for me being a miracle – an immediate, total
restoration of my body which would enable me to resume
normal operations at once.

First, there was that innate feeling common to mankind
that we ought to be well. The story is told of an old man
going to the doctor because of his increasingly gammy leg.
After the examination, the doctor said it was really just
due to age.

'Of all the reasons you could have given me doctor,' he replied, 'that one I know for sure to be wrong. I've had the other leg just as long and there's nothing wrong with it at all!'

In all of us, there remains the hint that we were intended to be immortal. Our bodies really ought not to go wrong, or wear out with age. The fact that they are incredibly complicated mechanisms seems almost beside the point. Yet to keep our 206 bones working requires 600 muscles. There are 300 million tiny air sacks in our lungs, the membranes of which if spread out would cover fifty-six square metres, provide oxygen for the six and a half litres of blood which has to be pumped round our body a thousand times a day. This depends on our lungs breathing in and out around a thousand times every hour and our heart beating thousands of times every hour. These are just a few of the staggering statistics that describe what it takes to keep our bodies functioning, which, until something goes wrong, we scarcely give a thought to.

There's even a sense of virtue in pushing our bodies to the limits. My aim as a forty-year-old was to try to live as if I were as fit as ever. Had I had a forty-year-old car, out of respect for the wear and tear it would have already endured, I would have avoided putting it through its paces too much. However, when it comes to our bodies, there's something within which suggests they ought to be exempt from the laws of nature we see applying to other mechanisms.

Then there is the in-built capacity of our flesh to heal. Even those who totally deny the reality of God recognize the healing properties of the human frame. Put the two parts of a broken branch of a tree together, and nothing happens. Put two broken bones together, and they not only have the potential to knit together as one, but can actually be stronger than if they had never been broken. Though the supernatural dimension to such healing may be denied, much confidence is still placed in the capacity

of our bodies to 'self-heal'. If they go wrong, we expect
them to get right again!

For those who know the reality of God as 'the Lord our
healer', that expectation can be even greater. We know
that a miracle is possible, and that the normal laws of
healing can be superseded. We know it can even happen
in an instant. We know God loves us, and cares about
that which afflicts us. Those of us who are parents know
how hard it can be to see our children suffer even slight
discomfort. How can our Father not be predisposed to
bring healing to His children at their point of need, right
NOW?

Such were my presuppositions in believing for healing.
Yet perhaps they would not have been so sharpened had
John Wimber not introduced to our shores a model of
healing which builds anticipation that God can heal
now. Those who have witnessed his conferences are left
in little doubt that where there is such expectation, God
does indeed do some spectacular things right now.

Certainly it's a message Western Europe has needed to
receive to shake us out of our rationalism. It has needed
go-getting, risk-taking Californians to wake us up to the
reality of God's power to intervene in our lives in dramatic
ways. Perhaps we have even needed an over-emphasis on
power healing in order to establish in us any emphasis on
it. However, I began to wonder about the danger of this
being the one and only frame of reference for our understanding of how God heals, such that anything which does
not deal with the obvious symptoms right now is less than
the best. This is not what John Wimber would say, but it
is all too easy to reduce what he is saying down to this.

Much as I had valued his teaching, I could not help
reflecting on the fact that he comes out of an extremely
'now' society, encapsulated in the bumper sticker which
said 'Eat dessert first – life is uncertain!' I began to see
the need to distinguish in what John Wimber has given to
us between what is kingdom, and what is purely a reflection of the culture he comes from. It raised the question

of whether we should have different presuppositions for the 'now' of the power evangelism situation, and for the long-term journey of the believer. Unfortunately, to open myself to such possibilities meant the willingness to let go of faith for 'an immediate total healing'.

The weight of the God who waits

Despite it being far more attractive to believe that God is primarily the One who acts 'now', what cannot be avoided in considering the overview of Scripture is how much He is also the God who waits. Indeed this is where the weight of emphasis mostly lies.

We read of how at Sinai He intervened in a moment with such mighty power and presence that the earth, the mountains and all the people of Israel trembled (Exodus 19:16–18). We read of how the 'shekinah' glory of God filled Solomon's temple at its dedication, such that even the priests could not get in because the presence of God was so great (2 Chronicles 7:2). Yet such 'theophanies', the manifestation of God's presence in the here and now, are the exception in Scripture, not the norm. More common is the type of story exemplified by Abraham, whose *cri de coeur* was 'How much longer must I wait to see God accomplish that which He promised?'

Examples abound. Joseph had to wait many years before he saw the fulfilment of the promise given to him as a boy. Moses was kept waiting forty years after having killed the Egyptian, an act he would surely not have committed unless the need for the Hebrews to be delivered was not extremely urgent. When he eventually got into business with Pharaoh, there was then the most protracted saga of plagues. Even the word of God for when they reached the promised land was that though He would drive out the Hivites, Canaanites and Hittites, it would not be in a year, but only 'little by little'; not until the Israelites had increased enough to take the land

(Exodus 23:30). That, of course, only began to happen after forty years in the wilderness.

Later followed many protracted years for the people of Israel as they first sought to live in the land under the admonition of the prophets, and then spent seventy years in exile. After this came the inter-testamental period between the last of the prophets and the coming of the Messiah. Why did He not intervene more quickly? Why indeed did He not act to force the people of Israel to respond in a way which was more honouring to Him? Even more importantly, what agony did God endure in watching His precious yet wayward children not heeding His desire to bring healing to them? We cannot tell. All we know is that this is our God.

God is evidently the One who waits. He waits because He loves us too much to always act in the here and now. Furthermore with Him, waiting time need not be wasted time. His desire is for our hearts to be prepared for His purposes. This may be blocked because of our sinfulness, but sin may not be the issue. It may be that a work is to be done in our hearts which can only happen with the passing of time. Jesus Himself had to wait until He was thirty before those three brief years of public ministry could begin. We may not understand God's timing but the fact is that 'The Lord is not slow in keeping his promise, as some understand slowness. He is patient . . .' (2 Peter 3:9).

It is our impatience that colours our understanding of slowness. It may well be that it is the roots of our impatience which need dealing with first, if we are to tune in to the way that God, who is willing to wait, desires to bring His deepest healing.

Though we are not in the 'now' culture of southern California, we still live in a credit card society, that associates with 'taking the waiting out of wanting'. When we want healing for ourselves or others, our impatience puts on the pressure to take the waiting out of it. Humanly, we may have some very good reasons for wanting to see that healing quickly. The difficulty is that such desire for speed may not always be in tune with the nature of the God from whom we seek that healing. He is the One who bears with agony. He is the One who is willing to wait until there is the willingness to seek His agenda before our own, to seek the restoration He wants to bring on His terms, rather than on ours.

From our viewpoint it may well feel that we're having to wait for God to catch up with us. With the psalmist we may want to cry out 'How long, O Lord? Will you forget me for ever? How long will you hide your face from me?' (Psalm 13:1). Perhaps even to have the brashness to say 'Awake, O Lord! Why do you sleep? Rouse yourself!' (Psalm 44:23). It seems as if precious time is being wasted. Yet though we have no perception of it, time may be being put to the best possible use. Through God's apparent lack of response, we may come to recognize that the invitation is in fact for us to catch up with Him, and not the other way round.

David's words in Psalm 40 testify, albeit in retrospect, to God's healing mercy. God lifted him out of the slimy pit, out of the mud and mire, set his feet on a rock, and gave him a firm place to stand. A new song was put in his mouth, a hymn of praise to God, that was to cause many to put their trust in the Lord. Yet he chose to begin the psalm with the words 'I waited patiently for the Lord . . .'.

God's heart for healing

If you're stuck in the mud, struggling to get out by yourself may simply get you in deeper. Isaiah reflected God's heart for us in writing 'In quietness and trust is your strength, but you would have none of it' (Isaiah 30:15). When we're in a mess the need to wait for the God who waits exposes where our faith truly lies. Wanting God to act in the here and now and heal dramatically may seem the most faith-filled approach there is. Deeper faith is however reflected by the psalmist who wrote 'I am still confident of this: I will see the goodness of the Lord in the land of the living. Wait for the Lord; be strong and take heart and wait for the Lord' (Psalm 27:13–14).

It is choosing to be strong in the Lord as we wait for Him to act that can begin us on the process of catching up with Him, and discovering what His agenda is for us, which may far exceed our desire for a short-term rescue plan. Were God to act predictably, and were miracles available to order, there would be little motivation to seek after God in the places where we have never sought to meet with Him before. Certainly it may feel as if God is playing games with us, to not heal with consistency. Far from it, when we are left waiting because we do not know God in the moment, we can be sure His desire is for us to know Him in a far greater way than we have so far understood. In eternal terms, to grow to know the God who heals us is the greatest miracle of all, which from that perspective far surpasses any immediate blessing in this world, however spectacular.

Ultimately, God's heart is for total restoration of our relationship with Him as it was originally created to be. The nature of that relationship is all too easily forgotten. It was to have been a participatory relationship in the running of the world. A world which God had created and continued to sustain moment by moment, but which man could co-operate within as he chose. Glory was to be given to God on earth, not primarily by spectacular interventions from Him, but by the way man chose to run the world as an act of worship to his Creator.

A delightful illustration of this comes in the story of the godly townsman out on a country walk. Peering over a wall, he saw a country yokel tending a beautiful garden. 'Nice to see what you and the Almighty have accomplished together,' he said cheerily. 'Yer should 'ave seen what it was like when the Almighty just 'ad it to 'Imself,' the yokel replied grumpily!

Even after the Fall, God's heart was still for that same participatory relationship with man. God could have intervened to spectacularly heal the whole of the cosmos in one infinite, eternal miracle. Instead, His heart was to involve mankind in the processes of redemption, leaving him to respond if he chose to. Certainly God intervened, first in sending the prophets, and ultimately in sending Jesus Christ into the world. However, even the Incarnation, the central miracle of all, it was not an instant 'fix-it'. Jesus inaugurated the kingdom of God, but left it to mankind to choose to respond. Jesus performed miracles, but more as signs to be responded to rather than as solutions for people's needs.

It will not be until the return of Jesus Christ that there will be the absolute intervention that will bring about the making of all things new. Even then, God's intervention will be entirely on His terms, in how and when it will happen. To have expectation that healing should be primarily through miracles, which we can simply pray into being to suit our needs, is to be seeking something which is outside God's general plan for His relationship with mankind.

This does not mean that there will not be times where He does intervene with a miracle that can restore someone to fullness of health. It may be to bring someone to faith. It may be to deliver God's people from particular attack from the evil one. It may be as a result of the expulsion of a demonic spirit which was entirely to blame for the illness. However, in the overall balance of the ministry of healing our expectations should be for a reflection, not of sudden and spectacular interventions from God, which require nothing of us other than the receiving of them, but of His heart for participatory relationship with Him. Our heart may well be for immediate and miraculous release from our illness. Mine certainly was. We may rationalize it by saying that we only want a miracle for the glory of God. Yet God's purposes go far beyond our immediate comfort or His short-term reputation.

Such understanding of healing diminishes the basis for anticipating the miracles which we define as spontaneous restorations of health. Certainly, there is a sense in which all healing is miraculous, because it reflects the intervention of God to restore what is ill or broken. However, the possibility of miracles yielding sudden recovery of health, though existing in a mature ministry of healing, are not then the supreme goal. In fact this may be far more consonant with Scripture. The book of Acts compresses a story spanning many years into what only takes an hour or two to read. The incidence of miracles was probably much less frequent than our rapid reading of it would suggest. Indeed, if miracles happened with great frequency, they would cease to be miracles in the sense of exceptional, supernatural events which evoke a sense of wonder. A mature model of healing therefore requires a mature understanding of their place in Scripture.

Furthermore, it provides an interpretation of John 14:12 which can undergird our practice of healing. Whilst Jesus promised that we will do 'even greater things', it can leave us utterly mystified as to how we can do things which are greater in kind or number than Jesus did. It suggests a journey into the realm of the miraculous, the like of which we cannot imagine. If, however, we bring mature perspective to the place of miracles in the healing ministry, then we are released to look in another direction to interpret this promise of Jesus. The 'greater things' will not be in kind or number, but in their consequence. Jesus said 'You will do even greater things than these, because I am going to the Father.' After Jesus had died, risen and ascended, the disciples were in no doubt that He was God's eternal Son. What they were able to do in His name would reveal more about Jesus than Jesus' own works could, before the fullness of the victory of Calvary was seen.

The healing works we are called to are therefore not about miracles greater in quantity or quality than those of Jesus. They are, however, to facilitate the receiving of the depth of healing which only the ascended Lord Jesus can minister. There is a place for miracles in a mature ministry of healing, but they are not the goal, and cannot be worked up to order. Analysis of the results of Morris Cerullo's 'Mission to London' in June, 1992, showed that despite a £200,000 campaign, the promise that 'some will see miracles for the first time' was not easily substantiated by later research. What Cerullo has made clear is that the advertising of miracles in advance makes for publicity that can get a human response. What the results of the mission made clear is that it does not get quite the same response from God.

God's healing purpose is that our broken relationship with Him, in all its consequences, might be restored. It is that glory might be given to Him on earth, not through what He might do by way of spectacular interventions, but by what we might do through lives which worship Him in all their changing circumstances.

3

What Does God Most Want To Heal?

Reflecting on what might be a broader perspective of healing, I began to wonder whether the basic model of healing introduced by John Wimber was something of a mixed blessing. By keeping things simple, he has opened the door to a practical model of healing that is accessible to anyone who genuinely wants to get into the healing ministry. There is no question that many, many good things have resulted from it. However, there seems to be a downside to it as well which is its potential to lead us to assume we can know how to co-work with God. This is only one short step from believing we really know what God wants to do. Unfortunately, it doesn't seem to be that simple.

John Wimber never fails to emphasize the need to listen to what God is saying to us when we pray for healing. However, my endeavours to hear what God was saying about my healing only brought home to me more of the unknowability of the God to whom we are supposed to be listening. Given the very limited track record we actually do have for healing, particularly for physical healing, I increasingly questioned the possibility of our truly hearing from God about what He most wants to heal.

However, through one little Hebrew word, the word 'yada', my hope was renewed. 'Yada' is used in Hebrew both of a man knowing his wife, and for someone knowing God. The paradox of marriage is that however much we become one flesh, our partners remain 'other'. Marriage is one long encounter with 'otherness'! Yet this does not stop us experiencing great energy of relationship in the early stages of knowing one another. Neither does it stop us from expecting to draw into deeper and deeper relationship with our partners, to get to know them better and better, and increasingly to enjoy contentment with them. Indeed it is in this journey that more mature energy of relationship is to be found, despite the unchanging dynamic of otherness.

So it is with knowing God. In the early stages of relationship with Him, though our knowledge of Him may be shallow, there can be great energy in it. We may have powerful 'now' experiences of God, which are completely genuine even though we scarcely know Him. The on-going experiences of God are, however, only really to be found in pressing forward in knowing Him, seeking to understand ever more of where He is coming from, despite it being a journey we can never complete on earth.

If we do press on to grow in *'knowing the unknowable'* as Paul puts it, then God's agenda can become more open to us. However it is likely to become less straightforward the further we progress. Inevitably it will touch us more and more in the depths of our being rather than in the superficiality of our doing, thereby touching the tension within us between being and doing.

Socrates' view of it was that 'to be is to do', Jean Paul Sartre by contrast considered that 'to do is to be', whilst Frank Sinatra managed to reconcile their differences by singing 'do-be-do-be-do'! Unfortunately, it usually takes more than a song to reconcile our differences with God over what is more important, our doing or our being. It's almost instinctive to judge the measure of healing we have received – be it naturally, through medicine, or through prayer – by whether the function we have lost has been restored. Yet this would not always seem to be God's criterion for healing. God may well want to change the balance of our being and doing into something which in His sight is much more whole, but which may not be our preferred choice. Worse still, He seems to regard it as worth paying a price for!

To respond to such healing ultimately requires a willingness to engage with the otherness of the God who, despite all He has achieved and done in creation, describes Himself primarily in terms of His being. When asked by Moses what he should say to the people of Israel was the name of the God who had sent him, He replied 'I AM WHO I AM'. Our names, or titles, are so often derived from what we do. However, the supreme Doer, who created a universe which modern-day science suggests could contain over 100 billion galaxies, chose to entitle Himself in terms of His being, rather than doing.

By contrast, we draw our sense of identity, and being, to a large extent from what we do. When we lose the capacity to do any of the key activities of our lives, be it through illness, accident, unemployment, change of circumstances or whatever, then the reality of the 'hole in the soul' that exists in us becomes more exposed. Such exposure can be very painful, and may well explain our foremost desire for the restoration of our capacity to do – so that the pain of that hole can be reduced once more through our achievements. 'To be or not to be' is a tough question we may be well-practised at avoiding answering.

Yet to grow in knowing the God who heals is to grow in knowing the One who is utterly complete in His sense of being. His desire to heal the bodies He has so 'fearfully and wonderfully made', as the Authorized Version of Psalm 139 puts it, is beyond our ability to comprehend. Yet His nature suggests that His desire to heal and restore our sense of being is far greater. How much we discern of the healing that God truly wants to bring depends on our willingness to face the painful exposure of what most needs healing in us.

In the final analysis, it hinges on the personal vulnerability, not only of ourselves, but also of God.

Jesus: the bearer of our healing

The Gospels reveal how Jesus brought healing to us as a
two-stage process. Firstly, it was through His words and
works. The kingdom was announced through what Jesus
did. Blind eyes were healed, the lame walked, demons
were driven out and the dead brought back to life. The
ways Jesus ministered healing varied. Sometimes it was
with a word or a touch. Other times even included the
use of saliva or mud. Whatever the means, in each case,
Jesus was the initiator, the One who healed others.

Yet none of the Gospels reach their conclusion without
making a massive transition. They start with Jesus as
the subject, the One who is 'done to'. As W. H. Vanstone
points out in *The Stature of Waiting*[1] it is when Jesus was
'handed over', that the transition is made from action to
passion. Only then is the way truly paved for Him to bring
the fullness of the healing He had come to bring.

When Jesus was the subject, though His healing
had great impact on those it touched, it was only the
announcement of the kingdom of God. The true locus of
healing was the cross, where Jesus was not the subject,
but the object of what happened. There the One who was
the exact representation of God's being allowed Himself
to be 'done to', that healing for a broken world might be
secured.

On the cross, Jesus made vulnerable not just His capacity to do, but His very being. For our sake, He became sin.
The One who was utterly complete in His being allowed
Himself to be changed, that we might have access to His
being in our lives. Yet despite our testimonies about how
much we appreciate what He did for us, we resist His
touch on the depths of our being. We are reluctant to let
Him change us too much, let alone deal with the deeper
aspects of the hole in our soul. Yet we may urgently desire
healing for whatever incapacitates us as doers.

Denial of the issues of our being, as long as they
don't too much affect our capacity for doing, can be

second nature, as can be the denial of our denial. We really don't want that hole in our soul to be probed any more than necessary. We do not naturally make ourselves vulnerable despite the vulnerability of Jesus on the cross.

However, to engage with the otherness of God in healing means to enter in to what it meant for the almighty, sovereign God who sits enthroned above the circle of the earth (Isaiah 40:22) to make Himself vulnerable. He is the God who is transcendent – over and beyond the created order. In no sense is He dependent upon it. He does not need the world in order to exist. The theological complexities of what it means for the transcendent God to choose to make Himself vulnerable are best left to the experts. What is simpler to see is that to make our being vulnerable to God is to put ourselves in line with the way He has primarily chosen to minister healing.

This suggests that in God's sight the healing of our being is more important than that of our body alone. It reflects an even greater revelation of God's nature than the disclosure of His capacity to do, which the whole of creation speaks about. The greater revelation is that God's capacity for being exceeds even that of His capacity for doing. It was this which led to His making Himself vulnerable to fallen mankind. In the process of healing, our growing to know more of this is a far higher priority to God than the restoration of our faculties to do the things we used to do.

Instantaneous healings can cause us to be amazed at God's capacity to touch us at our point of need. However, they do not necessarily take us any further in growing to know God. He loves us too much to leave us without the prompts to open up our perception of this. In His infinitely gracious mercy, God may therefore allow some limitation in our capacity to do which may even be permanent and which touches us for real. It is to remind us of just how different the priorities of God for healing can be from our own.

A painful healing at Jabbok

The story in Genesis 32 of what happened to Jacob at Jabbok is a classic illustration of God's different priorities. It was over twenty years since he had fled from his brother's anger. In that time God had blessed him with family and possessions, but the time had come to return, and the lifelong characteristics of Jacob the schemer came to the fore. With the memory of Esau's anger still vivid in his mind, he decided to send messengers ahead to allude to his riches and to seek favour with him. However the word was that Esau was coming to meet him with four hundred men, which caused great fear and distress for Jacob.

In panic Jacob acted in the hope that he might minimize what was to come. He sent his two wives, his two maidservants, his eleven sons, together with all his possessions, across the ford of Jabbok. It was night. He was totally alone. He had come to the end of himself. Here it was that he wrestled with the mysterious representative of God.

What happened at Jabbok had remarkable parallel to the wrestling that Jacob had been involved with in the dark of his mother's womb. The consequence of that first wrestling match was that, despite having been promised God's blessing, he never understood how to live in the promise of it. His life was built on seeking to secure blessing by manipulation, through his own ingenuity. Though apparently he had won, he had never been able to enjoy his victory over Esau. He had never obtained the sense of being that God had wanted to give him. He was insecure. He did not know how to receive, or be confident of God's ability to act on his behalf.

The turning point came in the wrestling match at Jabbok when it was clear that Jacob would not be overpowered. It was then the socket of Jacob's hip was touched, so that his hip was wrenched. Only when this had happened did Jacob say 'I will not let you go unless you bless me'. Blessing had always been what Jacob by his own scheming and ingenuity had sought to secure. Now, in the face of being at least to some extent incapacitated, possibly in pain, he recognized that blessing was something which may be sought, indeed held out for, but in the final analysis may only be received as a gift.

The fact that Jacob was not overpowered at Jabbok is a picture of the whole of his preceding life. God could have overpowered him at any time, as He can with any of us at any time. Yet despite all that we do to God to grieve Him, He continues to respect our dignity. He does not overpower us at the price of superseding our free will. Beyond this boundary He does not step. He may permit that which will prompt us to exercise our free will differently, but He leaves the choice with us. Its significance may have been greater in what it symbolized to Jacob rather than what it physically did to him, but nonetheless it was when his body was hurt that he changed. It was here that the transformation of his being began.

As he answered the question of what his name was, he effectively had to admit that he had been living up to what the name Jacob meant – supplanter. This was the character of his being. The blessing God wanted to give him as he lay there with his wrenched hip was a new name that would speak of a new sense of being. The new name was to be Israel, which speaks of one who has power with God.

The consequence of the injury in the wrestling match was a changed Jacob, who let go of his scheming, and simply limped towards his brother Esau, bowing seven times before him as they approached each other. What had gone on for Esau we do not know, but he came with forgiveness for Jacob. Forgiveness which the changed Jacob was now able to receive, such that the healing of his being was deepened yet further. Later we see Jacob's ability to pass on blessing as gift for others, to his sons and even to Pharaoh (Genesis 47:7,10).

Whether it was for the rest of Jacob's days, or only for a season, that he walked with a limp we don't know. Evidently the physical impact on him of that wrestling match made a great impression on those around him, such that it became a tradition not to eat the tendon attached to the socket of the hip because of how Jacob's hip had been touched. They wanted to remember the physical means God used to bring about the transformation of Jacob through the healing of his being.

God's priorities in healing

In our functional, 'now' society, our desire for physical health and the capacity to do can blind us to the lack of health we have in our inner being. Yet if we resist God's opportunities for Him to bring healing to our inner selves, we should not be surprised if He allows us to be touched at the place which will truly cause us to give Him our ear. His heart is to bless us, and to make us channels of that blessing to others.

As the story of what happened at Jabbok suggests, such blessing, which is about God's glory in us and through us, may indeed be better able to flow through bodies which are not completely whole, yet which contain inner beings that have truly been renewed. Henri Nouwen writes in *The Wounded Healer* 'Making one's own wounds a source of healing, therefore, does not call for a sharing of superficial personal pains but for a constant willingness to see one's own pain and suffering as rising from the depth of the human condition which all men share.'[2] It is the first-hand knowledge of God's capacity to minister healing right into the very depths of that condition which enables us to be ministers of healing to others.

The story of Susan James in *Healed Within*[3] is a graphic example of this. Her operation to remove a brain tumour left her paralysed, aged twenty-nine. Though not physically healed, she now displays a radiance that reflects the extensive healing of her damaged inner being. God's glory shines through her, and touches many as a result. All because of her conversion through a man called Geoffrey, who because of muscular dystrophy had been bed-ridden since the age of nine. Yet from his lips came the words of life which were to transform Susan.

His beaming face and sparkling blue eyes, his staggering knowledge of wild life, history, the arts, politics and religion, his sense of humour. Life evidently had abounded in that crippled body. What touched her most was his capacity to bring God into every conversation, in a spirit of constant thankfulness. At his funeral, amidst the mourning of his passing, the truth dawned. She saw written across the faces of those who had loved him, not desolation, but confidence. Confidence in the reality of eternal life. From there on, her own journey of healing, of spirit and soul, if not of body, began.

What the modern-day stories of Susan and Geoffrey point to is the same as that which Jacob's limp points to. There is a greater healing than that of the capacity to again do what we would regard as normal. It is the healing of that which is abnormal in our being, which is not shaped in His likeness. If we approach healing from the perspective of our 'now' society, which puts such high emphasis on functionality, and on the freedom to do what we want, whilst turning a blind eye to all that we inwardly suppress, then we may well end up with a different agenda from the God of eternity.

We may still seek to usurp the blessing of God by insisting on our own agenda, but as Jacob discovered, God cannot be obligated to do what we want. Our agenda may be good, but the good can be the enemy of the best. It is therefore not only ourselves, but also the simpler presuppositions for healing we would prefer to have, that we have to make vulnerable to God if we are to know what only He can give.

Going forward to be prayed for at a church where I was unknown, I was taken aback by a picture given through a man who I only had the chance to give the barest outline of my physical condition to. 'In what is happening to you,' he said 'God wants to change you from a trumpet into a harp. Does that mean anything to you?' It certainly did to my wife, Françoise, as I related the story to her later on. In the years since we met, she felt I'd made some progress from being brash to being brass, but the transformation from brass to strings would be equally desirable! It was the realization that God wanted, amidst all that was going on for me, to bring healing to my being, even ahead of my body, that began to change my conversation with God.

Was it a coincidence, I later wondered, that soon after this came the first sign, admittedly only slight, that the sarcoidosis in my body was beginning to remit?

4

Can Illness Be Explained Simply?

Impotent. This one word summed it all up. Having never before been signed off ill for a single day, the need for an extended period of rest left me feeling powerless.

However, the feeling was not totally new. I thought back some years to the failure of a business I had been setting up. In my youthful enthusiasm I had perhaps been naive about the commercial realities of importing Japanese wheelbarrows – but it was not without potential. What had happened seemed 'unfair', not because there is an inbuilt law of fairness in the commercial world, but because I had prayed hard about the whole venture. I had long dreamt of my own business through which to support Christian work, but had no desire to proceed with it, if it were not God's will. I had concluded the Lord was prompting me to go ahead – only for it to result in financial loss and bewilderment. Had I totally misread God's leading, or was the consequent powerlessness I found myself in part of a greater plan for my life?

A picture given to a Christian businessman who prayed with me about it spoke of God's power to bring good out of bad circumstances. He saw me as a little boy walking down a road, with my hand in my father's hand. I was used to holding his hand with the sense of warmth and security it gave. So much so that I didn't consciously feel my hand in his. Suddenly I tripped over a paving stone. I thought I was going to fall flat on my face and that it was going to hurt a lot. Only then I found not just the warmth and security of my father's hand, but also its strength. I felt a pull on my arm that hurt a little, but I discovered my father's power to save from what can really hurt.

These certainly transpired to be prophetic words. In the following months amazing things happened and I did indeed discover the strength of my Father's hand. I now look back to that time of powerlessness as a turning point in my life. However, the question remained, whether God in His mercy had simply redeemed what had happened to me, or was it that He had positively allowed me into a situation in order to change things in my life that could not be changed otherwise? I would happily have chosen the latter, except for one problem. Aspects of the 'unfairness' of what caused the failure of the business were not morally neutral. They were bad in God's sight. Surely God would not permit bad things to happen to us to accomplish His kingdom purposes in our lives?

Some questions in life are best put on the shelf, that we may get on with other things. Suddenly however, it was as if this one had, of its own accord, fallen off the shelf onto my lap, demanding to be faced. Now it centred around illness. Would God use illness as His means of shaping us afresh? Having been so encouraged by John Wimber's teaching on 'power healing', such a possibility cut in a very unacceptable direction.

The model of healing John Wimber has presented is of Jesus coming into this world as the 'divine invader'.[1] Satan is the prince of this world (John 14:30), and it is his kingdom of darkness in which sin and sickness roam freely, into which the Light of this world has come. The reason why the Son of God appeared was to destroy the devil's work (1 John 3:8). We look to the eschatological perspective of all things being made new, when sin and sickness will be no more. Meanwhile in this present evil age, we look for the in-breaking of the kingdom of God, the evidence of the age to come. It is both now and not yet. Our task is to be channels through which the greater power of Jesus can overthrow the power of the devil. This is that we might have more of the 'presence of the future' to borrow George Ladd's elegant phrase. The conclusion is, therefore, that where we see evil circumstances or sickness, our goal is to be used of God to eliminate them. Within this model there would thus appear to be no place for God to use illness for His kingdom purposes.

It was not only my own circumstances that had brought me to question whether there is not, however, a broader perspective on how God heals. I thought of a gifted, young pastor who had just gone through a year's illness. During this time he had scarcely been able to work. Yet his reflection in retrospect on what had been such a gruelling experience was that it was one of the best experiences of his life. God had done profound things in him that probably could have happened no other way. In his case it was the presence of circumstances that could not be overcome, in the form of physical illness, that was essential for a deeper healing to take place. If his and my circumstances were in some way from God, two questions followed. Does God initiate such a process, or just grasp His opportunity when He has it? Secondly, if we find ourselves in such a situation, how do we know what to resist and what to run with?

To tackle such questions requires some understanding of how God moves in the circumstances of life. I began to see that the view we have greatly influences the approach we take to the healing ministry. How we pray depends on whether or not we unreservedly see all apparently bad circumstances, especially illness, as something that cannot in any respect be of God, and which therefore need to be overcome as quickly as possible. It is a very different style of prayer that results from an openness to a bigger purpose of God, which somehow accommodates God not only redeeming bad circumstances, but perhaps even permitting some of them.

The first approach is attractive for its simplicity. However, its interpretation of God's dealings with His people does not appear sufficient for a more mature model of healing. The second gives a wider perspective on healing.

Unfortunately, it can diminish faith for dramatic release from illness. Given that we still so need our faith built up for the possibility of healing, this may not seem a good direction to pursue. It also promises theological difficulties that will not be easily reconciled. Yet, the discovery of new territories only happens when curious explorers take risks. If we are to draw a bigger map of healing, then some bold exploration is perhaps needed of how God may use apparently 'bad' things for His purposes.

Where our circumstances come from

Quite different reasons can be given to explain why things happen to us which we do not perceive as good. Some we bring upon ourselves, through our own sin. It may be accidental sin, which the Bible calls transgression. We have crossed the line by accident into a place we should not be. We didn't intend to, but no one else is to blame, and we have to bear the responsibility of it. Alternatively, it may be wilful sin – described in the Bible as iniquity. We deliberately chose to do what we did. We deluded ourselves into thinking there would be no consequence, but it rebounded, and we have to bear the brunt for what we chose to do. It is only when we humble ourselves in repentance before God for the hurt we have caused to Him and to others, that redemption of the hurt we have caused to ourselves can begin. Indeed, according to James 5:16, confession of our sins is a basic prerequisite for such healing.

Bad things can however be brought on us by others through their transgression or iniquity. Forgiveness can be hard, but without it, roots of bitterness can become established within us. These roots can be like mint planted in a garden, which can spread so rapidly, but can be so difficult to get rid of later. Redemption only begins as the choice to forgive is made.

Things also happen to us simply because we are unavoidably a part of a fallen world, where bad things happen to good and bad alike. God equally lets the rain and wind fall on the houses built on the rock as on those built on the sand. Faith-filled pragmatism, and the giving of thanks in the style of Habakkuk is the seed-bed of redemption for the catastrophes of this world. 'Though the fig-tree does not bud and there are no grapes on the vines, though the olive crop fails and the fields produce no food, though there are no sheep in the pen and no cattle in the stalls, yet I will rejoice in the Lord, I will be joyful in God my Saviour' (Habakkuk 3v17–18).

There is remarkable power over the destructive effect of circumstances when glory is consistently given to God regardless of whether things are going marvellously or disastrously. That tracing of the rainbow through the rain is described by George Matheson in his poignant hymn 'O Love that wilt not let me go'. It speaks of God's capacity to transform the downpour into something beautiful that reflects His eternal covenant of faithfulness. The rainbow is a wonderful symbol of the psalmist's testimony that 'In your light we see light' (Psalm 36:9). It is so real in its overarching shape yet it can never be reached and touched. It is impossible to get hold of a piece of rainbow to prove the reality of it to a sceptic who has never seen one. God's overarching promise, real as it is, is there only to the eye of faith that comes alive through worship.

Repentance, forgiveness, worship. Once we can get beyond the emotions which go with the experience of apparently bad things, we can be clear that there are God-given channels through which redemption of what has happened can be received. However, what complicates matters is that there are also supernatural explanations for our circumstances, for which the appropriate response is less easily discerned.

The fact is that bad things can happen to us because of the sheer malevolence of the evil realm, which we need to resist. The devil will attack us with his flaming arrows, and we are warned in the famous passage on spiritual armour in Ephesians 6 to be ready to take up the shield of faith with which they can all be extinguished. Some bad things evidently originate not with our sin or anyone else's, nor even in realities of living in a world where things go wrong. The devil has his schemes. 'Our struggle is not against flesh and blood, but against the rulers, against the authorities, against the powers of this dark world and against the spiritual forces of evil in the heavenly realms' (v12). At least some of what happens to us comes from this direction. We must not be naive about it. Against it we must stand firm, and make a robust defence.

What we must not resist however is the discipline God wants to minister to us through the circumstances we face. Here we need to cooperate with what is going on, even though it may not be a comfortable experience. The writer to the Hebrews urges his readers not to forget that word of encouragement addressed to all who are God's children: 'My son, do not make light of the Lord's discipline, and do not lose heart when he rebukes you, because the Lord disciplines those he loves, and he punishes everyone he accepts as a son' (Hebrews 12:5,6).

The writer goes on to speak of the need to endure hardship as discipline, and to recognize that if we have no experience of being disciplined by God, it raises questions about the authenticity of our sonship. No father who loves his children leaves them undisciplined. God's discipline is for our good, that we might share His holiness, yet no matter how tremendous its ultimate purpose, like all earthly discipline, at the time it will seem painful. Unless we are masochists, such pain will not feel good. What God chooses to discipline us with could well feel bad, yet it is that with which we are to co-operate.

The experience of refinement develops this further. To the suffering church Peter wrote to, he says of the trials they faced: 'These have come so that your faith – of greater worth than gold, which perishes even though refined by fire – may be proved genuine and may result

in praise, glory and honour when Jesus Christ is revealed'
(1 Peter 1:7).

Though it was into a particular situation of suffering
that Peter was writing, the general principle of the Lord
coming as a refiner is prophesied by Malachi. 'He will
be like a refiner's fire or a launderer's soap. He will
sit as a refiner and purifier of silver; he will purify
the Levites and refine them like gold and silver . . .'
(Malachi 3:2–3).

This prophecy looks to the day of judgment, but it
nonetheless reflects the nature of God who uses fire to
burn off the dross even as John the Baptist prophesied:

> 'I baptise you with water for repentance. But after
> me will come one who is more powerful than I, whose
> sandals I am not fit to carry. He will baptise you with
> the Holy Spirit and with fire. His winnowing fork is
> in his hand, and he will clear his threshing floor,
> gathering his wheat into the barn and burning up
> the chaff with unquenchable fire.'
>
> (Matthew 3:11,12)

If we believe the baptism of the Holy Spirit is to be
received as a present experience, then the words of John
the Baptist suggest the baptism of refining fire must also
be received as a present experience.

In my days in the foundry industry, it was fascinating
to see the amount of dross which had previously been
imperceptibly distributed within an ingot of metal that
could be brought to the surface as it was heated up. With
care it could then be skimmed off, leaving the metal purer
and of greater worth. When God refines us, it is a different
process from disciplining. It is not about the dealing with
our weaknesses but with the bringing out of our potential.
To be refined is the affirmation that we have within us
something which is worth refining. It is the quality of
what lies within which is being primarily looked at, not
the presence of that which will form the dross.

Yet as metal is melted in order to be refined, it first loses resilience, and then its shape. It becomes fluid and vulnerable. So it is with us when we are being refined. We may with sincere heart sing of our desire to be purified, to be as gold and silver, and yet refinement means a journey into the heat, and into the place of vulnerability. We cannot be refined and maintain our resilience at the same time. We simply have to entrust ourselves to the Refiner through what may seem a far from good experience.

The picture of the Father as the gardener who prunes the branches of the vine makes the same point. Even a branch that is fruitful 'he prunes so that it will be even more fruitful' (John 15:2) because His purpose through us is that we bear fruit that will last (v16). Pruning is about the experience of being cut back. In the short-term it does not feel like a good experience.

Scripture also gives examples of God's purpose being accomplished through the use of agencies which are not good. For example, Judges 9:23 describes how God sent an evil spirit for the accomplishment of His purposes, between Abimelech and the citizens of Shechem who had acted treacherously against him. Isaiah 45:1 speaks of King Cyrus as His anointed, yet there is no evidence that Cyrus worshipped God, only that God had chosen to use him for His purposes. Acts 8:1 describes a great persecution which caused the scattering of the believers. Yet it was to be crucial to the spread of the gospel by the early church to fulfil Jesus' promise in Acts 1:8 that they would be witnesses beyond Jerusalem, to Judea and Samaria and to the ends of the earth.

Paul through his 'thorn in the flesh' which he described as 'a messenger of Satan' (2 Corinthians 12:7) had personal experience of how God could use what was bad in itself for the advancement of His purposes. Through it Paul grew in his understanding of how God's strength is made perfect in weakness. Yet for him it was torment – expanded in the Amplified Bible as 'to rack and buffet and harass'. This was on top of the catalogue of all the other hardships he had endured, described in 2 Corinthians 11:23–28.

The crushing of lavender to yield its fragrance, or of an orange to yield its juice, are pictures of how even in nature that which is good requires an apparent process of destruction that it might be released. Paul spoke of rejoicing over the spiritual equivalent of this because of the chain of good response that can lead to a developed understanding of the hope of the glory of God. 'We know that suffering produces perseverance; perseverance, character; and character, hope. And hope does not disappoint us . . .' (Romans 5:3–5).

A 'bad' circumstance could therefore be that which the Lord might be wanting to use for our discipline or refinement, or for the development within us of spiritual hope. Indeed even for the advancement of His purposes which we have no ability to comprehend from our viewpoint. God may actually want us to be overcome by it, that His purposes might be worked out in us or through us.

Where that which we may perceive as 'bad' comes from, could therefore be explained in different ways, calling for different responses. It could have identifiable natural origins which need addressing appropriately. However it could also be supernatural and rather less identifiable in origin. It could be the attack of the devil which must be resisted. Such circumstances must not be allowed to overcome us. It could be from God, with whom we are to co-operate. The interpretation of the circumstances of life, and the response they require is, unfortunately, no simple matter.

Can illness ever be from God?

How far then might this rather complex view of the origins of 'bad' circumstances in general apply to the experience of illness and disease in particular? Could they be a little simpler to interpret, given the black and white clarity of Deuteronomy 28:22 regarding sickness as being under the curse that follows from disobedience?

Certainly loss of health can come about through our own sin. We can transgress the line of what is healthy unintentionally by, for example, working too hard, and bearing both physical and psychological consequences as a result. We can also do it through iniquity. We may abuse our bodies deliberately, for example by smoking, hoping we will get away with it, only to find one day that it is too late. The man Jesus healed at the pool called Bethesda, who had been an invalid for thirty-eight years was told by Him to 'stop sinning or something worse may happen to you' (John 5:14). The Corinthian church was warned that unconfessed sin before taking communion had caused some to be weak and ill, and others even to fall into the sleep of death (1 Corinthians 11:30). The rapid spread of AIDS is perhaps today the sharpest reminder of how illness can spread through wilful, sinful action.

The sin of others, be it accidental or deliberate, can also cause loss of health. For example, dangerous driving by someone perhaps unknown to us can lead to injury of our body and even mind. It is simply the consequence of an interactive world of sinners, that the sins of one person can directly damage another, in body, soul or spirit. However, direct connection between illness and personal sin only explains a small part of the illness there is in the world.

It is the indirect consequence of sin having entered into this world which explains a much greater proportion of the world's lack of health. Whereas prior to the Fall creation was universally healthy, as sin entered into the world, it became universally unhealthy. Certainly there are geographical factors, such as with malaria which is rather more prevalent in the tropical rain forests of the world than in Western Europe. However, it is factors such as poverty and malnutrition which make illness vastly more prevalent in some parts of the world than in others. For example, whereas there is one doctor in Britain for

every 680 people, in Tanzania, it is one for every 34,000.
A child in the Third World averages an illness every three
weeks. Life expectancy in Nepal is just forty-six years.

There is also that dimension to the loss of health which
can strike anyone anywhere. The young mother with
small children is as vulnerable to cancer in one part
of the world as another. It is simply part of the fallen
nature of this world that none of us are immune from.
Commenting upon the eighteen who were killed when
the tower of Siloam fell upon them, Jesus said it was
nothing to do with their sinfulness, they were no worse
than anyone else (Luke 13:4). The fact that we get ill
may have nothing directly to do with our sinfulness, or
anyone else's. It could just be one of those things in the
world in which we live.

It could, though, be of the devil because illness is part
of his weaponry. It is part of the curse of his presence in
this world. The physical consequences for those delivered
by Jesus of demons were enormous. For example, the
healing in Matthew 12:22 of the demon possessed man
who was both blind and mute was not just about spiritual
deliverance. It was physical as well. The consequence
was that he could both talk and see. The use of the
identical word by Jesus in Luke 4 both to rebuke an
evil spirit (v35) as well as to rebuke the fever of Peter's
mother-in-law (v39) is evidence of how physical illness
can be demonically linked.

So far the explanation of where illness comes from
seems to fit into the general pattern of how 'bad' circumstances may be explained. To identify its origins may
therefore be far from simple, and the implication is that a
mature model of healing needs to be able to take account
of this. However, the biggest question of all is whether
the parallel pattern goes all the way. Do we need a
model of healing that can handle the possibility of illness
on occasion being from God? Certainly the accounts of
Daniel's visions suggest at the very least that illness can
be the consequence of spiritual vision sent by God. As a

result of visions given to him by God, he was rendered 'exhausted and lay ill for several days' (Daniel 8:27), with 'no strength left' and with his 'face turned deathly pale' (10:8) such that he could 'hardly breathe' (10:17).

My uncomfortable conclusion was that any model of healing which will stand the test of time will have to engage with the complex mystery of suffering.

5

Can There Be A Good Purpose In Suffering?

The tough question I increasingly faced was how one model of God's dealing with mankind could embrace both the promise of healing and the purpose of suffering. Does any area of overlap exist, or do we need two separate theologies? I reflected on what some think is the most ancient book of the Bible, to consider again the purpose of Job in Scripture.

Job was blameless and upright. He feared God and shunned evil (Job 1:1). However, the extent to which the devil was allowed by God to test him did not stop with the total loss of his possessions, his sons and his daughters. Ultimately he was permitted to put on to Job disease which only stopped short of that which would take his life. He was afflicted with painful sores from the soles of his feet to the top of his head (2:7).

What follows for the next thirty chapters is the attempt of Job's friends, Eliphaz, Bildad and Zophar, to interpret his suffering in terms of his sinfulness. After many words have been exchanged they retire from the scene having made no progress. Then comes Elihu with a slightly different approach. His thrust is not that God is the One who puts disease on to people to punish them for their sin, although his portrayal of God as teacher at places stops little short of this (33:16–22, 36:8–10). The breakthrough for Job on his subsequent restoration, comes, however, not through getting hold of the explanation behind what had happened to him, but through humbling himself before God. 'Surely I spoke of things I did not understand, things too wonderful for me' (42:3).

From the heavenly vantage point given at the start of the story we are permitted a perspective we do not normally have when sickness and suffering is encountered. It demonstrates that the experience of disease may have nothing to do with personal sinfulness – but can have its origin in the supernatural realm in ways totally beyond our understanding.

What the opening verses of the story describe is the complexity of the relationship between God and the devil which the natural mind cannot grasp. They begin with a conversation between God and the devil, in which it is God himself, who raises the question of Job and his uprightness. The devil's argument is that Job only worships God because he has been protected by Him, and if such protection were removed, Job would curse Him. God then permits the devil to touch any of Job's goods, but not to lay a finger on his person. The consequence is the loss of everything other than his wife and his health. Then the devil returns into the presence of God, and again it is God who raises the question of Job and his uprightness. This time the devil argues that if Job's life were threatened, then he would curse God. So he is given permission to do anything to the health of Job, short of taking his life, and from there the story develops.

Where this opening passage came from is indeed fascinating! Yet if our conviction is that all Scripture is inspired by God and profitable for teaching (2 Timothy 3:16), whatever its origins we cannot bypass the significance of such a substantial chunk of Scripture. The fact that the story of Job can't be fitted into a simpler understanding of the origin of sickness suggests that the simpler, more easily handled assumptions are inadequate.

The clear thrust of it is that God can initiate circumstances in which testing can come about, which can go as far as disease, and which the devil is allowed to bring upon people within the limits permitted by God. It also implies that this can happen even to the most upright. However difficult this is to rationalize from our viewpoint, it puts the experience of sickness into the context of an ever greater difficulty – the problem of theodicy, how the providential rule of God may be reconciled to the presence of evil in the world. If God created all things '*ex nihilo*', that is out of nothing, and if His eyes are too pure to look on evil (Habakkuk 1:13) then where did evil, including disease, come from? How can God allow good to come out of evil, be it sickness or any other form of bad experience?

Yet it is not just the story of Job which suggests that circumstances, including illness, may be allowed upon us which God can use for His purposes. Paul, in Galatians 4:13, reminds them that it was only because of his illness which had been a trial to them, that he first preached the gospel to them. That may be seen purely as God capitalizing on an opportunity. However, there is more specific evidence that some circumstances we encounter are those which are intended by the devil for evil, but out of which God intends to bring good. Joseph, following his reconciliation with his brothers in Egypt, said to them, regarding the way they had sold him for twenty shekels of silver to the Ishmaelites: 'You intended to harm me, but God intended it for good to accomplish what is now being done, the saving of many lives' (Genesis 50:20)

Of infinitely greater significance than the sparing of lives from starvation that Joseph was able to accomplish, was the salvation Jesus brought about. Peter spoke of it in his great Pentecost sermon like this: 'This man was handed over to you by God's set purpose and foreknowledge; and you, with the help of wicked men, put him to death by nailing him to the cross.' (Acts 2:23)

Here was the supreme demonstration that God sends His salvation through the self-same channels that the devil wants to use for evil. Behind what we may experience in the natural realm therefore can be an intertwining of purposes in the spiritual realm. This is not dualism, in which God and the devil with equal power battle it out, for the devil is no more than a fallen angel. God remains in absolute control. Yet what it faces us with is that God's saving purposes can in some way be worked out within the apparently 'bad' things which happen to us.

There is profound mystery in this. Job and Paul Simon may not at first sight appear to have much in common. The words though in Paul Simon's song 'Slip-Sliding Away' that 'God only knows, God makes his plan, the information's unavailable to mortal man' are ones that Job may well have echoed. Despite this, the inclusion of the story of Job in Scripture suggests some very important things. The interpretation of where bad things in general, and sickness in particular, come from is, in the final analysis, beyond us. Simple frames of reference for healing, though having a value, need to be put into this far greater context. Scripture therefore needs to be understood as much as a guide on how to handle hurt we do not understand as a manual for healing. Herein lies the overlap. What matters most is not the nature of the circumstance, but our stance in the face of it.

Overcoming evil with good

David Watson, facing the inoperable cancer that he was shortly to die of, wrote in *Fear No Evil*

> There are seldom good reasons for suffering, but there can be good responses ... As we learn to respond positively, however, we shall be able one way or another, to overcome suffering so that the explanation becomes no longer of major importance. Those who learn that lesson often achieve a remarkable quality of life that may be far in excess of the trouble-free existence of others. It is not what we do, but who we are that matters most in life; and it is not what we endure, but the way we endure it that counts. We can overcome evil with good.[1]

Though our prayer is always 'Your will be done on earth
as it is in heaven', this is something which may well be
far beyond our capacity to work out, however hard we
try. Whatever the interplay of good and evil, our task is
to look for the overcoming of evil with good, and to leave
the rest to God. The story of Alexander Solzhenitsyn is a
gripping example of what this can mean in practice. After
many years in the brutality of Stalin's prison camps, he
was able to say 'Bless you, prison, for having been in my
life'. Not in any sense was what had happened there good.
Yet with hindsight it was possible for him to see how, in
the evil of that prison experience, God had worked for
good both in him and through him. It might never have
happened any other way.

His story points to the huge difference between the
experience in the moment and in the overview. When
the news was broken to Winston Churchill that he'd lost
the post-war election with the words 'it may be a blessing
in disguise', he is supposed to have retorted 'Bloody good
disguise!' As Christians we might not select the identical
vocabulary, but we may well have the same sentiments
about the possibility of blessing ever resulting from what
is happening to us. Only later are we able to appreciate
the hand of the One whose only desire is to bless us, that
felt so disguised in the moment.

Shortly after moving into the house where I did my
first curacy, a well-meaning friend sent to me the words
of Psalm 25:10 'All the ways of the Lord are loving
and faithful for those who keep the demands of his
covenant'.

My immediate reaction was to try to work out where
I had been failing God in the demands of His covenant!
It had only been possible to secure a house in the area
we were to live in by taking the council house no one else
would touch. Just to open the front door was enough to put
off any would-be occupier. The stench practically knocked
me over. With my daughters then aged six months and
two years, I could scarcely believe that this was where

God wanted me to take them. The stories of what subsequently happened fill Françoise and me with amazement as we look back on those two years living there. At the end of it though, we were able to echo the words of the psalmist in a way that we would never have known had we not gone into that situation.

What determines whether our experience of suffering becomes a channel God works through is not primarily to do with the experience in itself. If suffering had any intrinsic benefit, the world would be full of people who by now would be vastly more whole than they are. It is up to us whether we allow suffering to make us, in John Wimber's words, 'bitter or better'. All it does is to confront us with the choice of how we will respond, and to give us the opportunity to grow into greater strength of being.

During his experience of being tortured by the Japanese during the Second World War, Leonard Wilson was asked why, as one who professed faith in God, God didn't save him. His reply was that 'God doesn't save people from punishment or pain. He saves them by giving the strength and the spirit to bear it'. After the war, he became Bishop of Birmingham. Part of his ministry was to return to baptize one of his torturers who had come to faith in Christ as a result of the faith and witness of Bishop Wilson during the war. Few of us will ever have to face the type of torture he endured, but that does not exempt us from the feeling of extremity of circumstance that can bring great despair.

One dark, misty night, feeling under pressure on many fronts, I drove out into the countryside to be with God. Primarily, I intended to vent my feelings to Him about all that was happening to me, without the embarrassment of the neighbours hearing. I left the car on the verge with only one sidelight working, and walked down the road through the thickening fog. A remarkable optical effect resulted from that one light shining from behind me into the fog ahead of me. Projected into the opacity that I was walking into was a huge silhouette of my figure. I felt the

Lord say to me 'What matters far more than the changing
of your circumstances is whether you are willing to be
changed through them, indeed to grow through them. I
have a much bigger picture of you that I want you to step
forwards into. But it's up to you whether or not you do.'

So much of what was going on was beyond my capacity
to change. The only thing I had some power to influence
was the response I would make to my circumstances.
This meant foregoing my desire for God to explain why
He allowed the things He did, as if He owed me at the
least an explanation, and preferably an apology. Instead,
humbly to seek to hear what He wanted to say to me. I
later realized that had it not been for the fog, that picture
resulting from the light shining from behind could never
have happened. The fog of my circumstances which I
could see no way though was the very screen on which
the Light could project what He wanted to do with me.
Without that screen, the picture could not be seen.

It set me thinking afresh of the words of Isaiah to the
people of Israel in their obstinacy:

> And though the Lord give you the bread of adversity
> and the water of affliction, yet your Teacher will not
> hide himself any more, but your eyes shall see your
> Teacher. And your ears shall hear a word behind you,
> saying, 'This is the way, walk in it,' when you turn to
> the right or when you turn to the left.
>
> (Isaiah 30:20–21; RSV)

What matters is not our theological or emotional wrangling
with God about why or how He might 'give' adversity or
affliction, but whether we will seek to hear and respond
to His word to us in the situation about how good might
be brought out of it.

This means accepting it as a reflection not on God's
nature but upon our own that we may need to be disabled
before we can be enabled in the way God would have us
be. We may need to recognise that this can be God's way

of answering our prayers to be more greatly used of Him.
As an anonymous author has put it:

I asked for strength – and God gave me difficulties
   to make me strong.
I asked for wisdom – and God gave me problems to
   learn to solve.
I asked for prosperity – and God gave me brain and
   brawn to work.
I asked for courage – and God gave me dangers to
   overcome.
I asked for love – and God gave me troubled people
   to help.
I asked for favours – and God gave me opportunities.
I received nothing I wanted; yet I received everything
   I needed.
My prayer had been answered.

Our lives, even in Christian ministry, can be wrapped up
in pushing so much towards goals which are not the ones
God is calling us to. We may be paying a heavy price to do
so, as may our families and others around us. Tragically,
those who do make it to the top of their chosen ladder
all too often discover it was up against the wrong wall.
Perhaps it is the subconscious realization of this which
prompts the maxim that 'it's better to travel in hope than
to arrive'.

It is because of the mercy of God that He is willing
to disable us in our ability to achieve our earthly goals.
What may seem so painful to us is the gift of the material
of re-evaluation. Through this we may hear a word in
our ear that we had previously been deaf to. It can
cause us to appreciate the anchor points in our lives
that God has already given us, that require no more
achievement for them to be enjoyed. Indeed a whole new
perspective can come about through such intervention of
God in our lives.

During a visit to a DIY store God spoke to me very

clearly about this. The tiredness I was struggling against
had become a major problem, but there was a practical
job which nonetheless had to be done. I felt angry towards
God that despite my tiredness, I had to push on with the
job. That is until I saw a man standing in front of me.
First it was his cheerful smile that touched me. Then
it was the realization that he had no hands – probably
a Thalidomide victim, judging by his age. What he was
doing in such a store I had no idea, because evidently he
had never in his life turned a screw-driver or wielded
a hammer. Things I loved to do and could do by reflex.
Subsequent reflection followed on many things I took for
granted without appreciating the worth of.

Indeed, it caused me to seek God afresh for what He
wanted to do through my life. Despite all my thinking
about the possible explanations for my illness, be it
sin, or just 'one of those things', be it spiritual attack
or God's refinement of me: whatever it might be – the
most important thing was to seize the opportunity for
change. Had I received the miracle I originally wanted,
and been healed immediately, I doubt if I would have
reached such a point. My conclusion was that God's hand
had evidently been in my experience of an illness which
was not immediately overcome by medicine or prayer. He
can indeed have good purpose in suffering.

Different wavelengths for healing

Given this experience as well as that of power healing,
the challenge was to find the common theology which does
justice to both. An apparently immense challenge indeed.

Within the power healing model the explanation of
'bad' things remaining after prayer, and the sick not
being healed, is the 'now and not yet' of the kingdom.
The healings we do see are understood as the signs
of the fullness of what is to come, the eschatological
prospect of all things being made new. They are like
the signs we see going down a motorway. There can be

large gaps in between where faith is required that we are still travelling in the right direction. However, they are located sufficiently often to keep us reassured, and indeed the nearer we get to our destination, the more relevant the signs become.

Such an understanding of healing as a sign of the kingdom of God allows for the presence of more suffering than healing, and the gaps between the times when we have clear evidence that we are going in the right direction. It also keeps open the possibility of a major sign of healing always being just round the next corner.

Thus far the power healing model has provided a scripturally valid basis for the ministry of healing, as well as explaining why we do not see all the healing we pray for. The tough question about it though is whether or not it reflects the fullness of what Scripture says about how God purposes to bring healing, particularly that He may even want to use what is 'bad' in order to bring about good. To immediately and miraculously remove the bad which the devil wants to use for evil certainly deprives him of his opportunity. This is a laudable goal in the power healing model. However, it can equally deprive God of His opportunity. John and Paula Sandford quote Bob Mumford as saying that 'if we fix the fix that God has fixed to fix a man, God will have to fix another fix to fix him.'[2] At this point there seems to be something of a hole in the power healing model.

However, to develop a mature model of healing which integrates both the principles of power healing as well as God's use of 'bad' circumstances is like trying to find one model which accommodates both the sovereignty of God and the free-will of mankind. Both are scripturally valid, yet to our limited minds, they pose apparently irreconcilable contradictions. We may, like the Arminians and the Calvinists, solve our problem by choosing to emphasize one view over and against the other. Or we may see the solution in a creative tension. Unfortunately, the latter tends to make us more tense than creative!

Nonetheless, in the new Jerusalem, the tree of life stands symbolically on both sides of the river of life (Revelation 22:2). The picture certainly poses problems for literalists, and perhaps it is meant to. It could be that it teaches us that in many fundamental areas of Christian truth we should not expect one model in which no literal contradictions exist. Yet it also teaches that there is the encouragement to believe that truth as it originates from the throne of God, from whence the river flows, simultaneously stands on both sides. Is the way forward therefore to seek not so much literal as visual expressions of the theology which unites the two understandings of how God may move in healing? The aim of such creative pictures would be to accommodate in a relaxed way both views of how God may want to bring healing, indeed to express how they may even complement each other?

One such picture is the analogy of a radio. Let us imagine power healing to be one wavelength. Reception, the equivalent to finding healing, may be found at different points on that wavelength as the tuner is adjusted. Substantial gaps exist in between. However, there is a second wavelength on the radio. What is received on it has a very contrasting sound, though it comes through the same receiver. Again reception exists at different points on the tuner with gaps in between. The characterstic of a radio is that where there is no reception on one wavelength, reception may be discovered by switching wavelengths without moving the tuner. It may have a very different sound to that which we would have preferred to hear. Yet it is still far better than nothing.

So this picture of different wavelengths of healing speaks of how they can co-exist. And it also suggests that God may even allow the tuner to get jammed by circumstances beyond our control to force us to explore the other wavelength of healing we might not like the sound of so much.

The use of such a picture may not seem to be profound

theology. Yet God chose the foolish things of the world to shame the wise (1 Corinthians 1:27). Perhaps it is that the profounder aspects of a more mature model of healing will need simple pictures through which it can be both expressed, and also received, by faith. The nature of that faith is, however, something we need to be most clear about.

6

What Is The Place Of Faith In Healing?

'We invite all who have any need of healing to come forward to be prayed for.' Nowadays, particularly since John Wimber's visits to this country, such a request is not unusual. However, this was pre-Wimber, and I was in a meeting organised by part of the American 'Faith Movement'. My only need of healing then was short-sightedness, and having got used to wearing glasses, it was not a big concern to me. What concerned me was learning about healing. I had become convinced that the church should be practising healing far more than it was, and the approach of the Faith Movement was a possibility to explore. So I plucked up my courage and went forward to see if my eyesight would be 'healed by faith'.

Panic hit me, however, as I watched the method used on the group ahead of me who had been lined up in a row across the stage. Gloria, the wife of Kenneth Copeland, who has been described as the 'heir apparent' to Kenneth Hagin in the American Faith Movement, swept past each one with the briefest of prayers. Like a row of dominoes, every single one of them went over in the Spirit. They were allowed to remain there for no more than a moment, before being yanked to their feet by a burly steward, and then immediately directed off the stage to make space for the next group to be 'done'. I'd never been slain in the Spirit and wasn't sure if I'd be able to respond as I ought to. I certainly didn't want the embarrassment of being the only one left standing, especially as it was being televised. On the other hand I didn't want to be filmed as the one who made the great escape!

Before I realized it, I had been up on the stage, prayed for, flat on my back, yanked up on my feet, ushered off the stage, and pointed back towards my seat. It was a strange experience to say the least. Watching it later on television, I was even more bemused by the whole thing. I wasn't pushed. The only conclusion could be that spiritual power was present to cause me, like the others, to fall over spontaneously as we were prayed for. However, if God could do that, why hadn't He healed my eyesight? Perhaps I had lacked real faith.

However, we were told that had we not received our healing we should still declare that we had. We should claim the full manifestation of it. We should live as if the healing had been fully completed. We should not work on the basis that 'seeing is believing', which is the way a faithless world thinks. Instead we should exercise the 'God type of faith' which declares that we believe first, and then we see the results of our faith. Our healing will come from the confession of our lips. If I had lacked faith in that meeting, I still had the opportunity to prove I was a man of faith.

Off went my glasses, and I vowed never to wear them again. Then followed my season of walking by faith rather than by sight, not just spiritually, but very literally! It can only be described as an extended journey of near collisions. Missing people in the street was to be regretted, whereas missing cars on the road was something to be thankful for. Looking back it was naive and dangerous. I would never recommend to anyone that driving without glasses is the way God brings about healing of eyesight. Having said that, there is something else I have to add. After three months, my eyesight began to improve, such that I've not needed glasses since! Perhaps there was a natural explanation as the muscles of my eyes were somehow strengthened by so much squinting. Perhaps God healed them directly, if only to preserve me from catastrophe. I shall never know. What I do know from first hand experience is something of the type of risk which can go with the Faith Movement approach to healing.

Risky faith

Given that supernatural healing depends on faith, and faith as John Wimber has repeatedly said, should be spelt r-i-s-k, the ministry of healing unavoidably involves venturing into the place of risk. In the place of that risk, however, lies many dangers. They extend as far as the possibility of abuse, and ultimately even of the devil taking over. For a mature ministry of healing to be developed, a clear understanding is needed of what sort of faith and risk God is calling us to, and what He is not. Unfortunately, as I grappled with this regarding my sarcoidosis, there was something I could not deny. God had already convinced me through personal experience that He does accomplish His purposes by taking His people into situations of high risk. Indeed through one in particular some years previously I had subsequently received much inner healing.

Sitting under a vine in the old city of Jerusalem on a scorching summer's day, I had found myself in conversation with a young French woman. It was the sort of thing that happens in the cosmopolitan atmosphere of Israel where the paths of Christians from all over the world cross. We spoke for a quarter of an hour or so during which she told me of the possibility of her coming to England the following autumn to go to Bible College. Providing God answered several prayers in a remarkable way, that was!

Six months later, through a common contact, we met again, this time in England. God had indeed answered her prayers quite amazingly. Once more, we only had a short time together, but we agreed that after I got back from a skiing trip, we would meet properly. I didn't then realize what 'proper' was to mean! However, amidst the grandeur of the Alps, I suspected God was saying that we would get married. Back in the damp cold of England I decided it was the rarefied air that had affected me – until the night before I was due to go and see her. Then I clearly heard God say we were to be engaged the next morning. It seemed ridiculous, having spent in total no more than an hour alone together. Yet God had said the same to her, and it was a *fait accompli* even before I was able to ask her formally.

Twelve years on, Françoise and I are happily married, and have mutually experienced much inner healing through our marriage. It was indeed God who had called us to take such a risk – the size of which I only began to realize later, since, as a clergyman, I have counselled couples in marital difficulty. Yet testimony of how God has moved, indeed even brought healing, as a result of His people taking substantial steps of faith, does not automatically mean that the more risk, the more it must be real faith, which God is increasingly bound to honour.

Spirit-given discernment is needed to know the difference between the various types of risky faith we can become involved with. It may be faith God is calling us to which could go far beyond anything that we might ever think or imagine. It may be humanly inspired faith, from that which is simply misguided through to that which ultimately seeks to manipulate God. It may even be that which the devil has lured us into, through which he seeks some form of opportunity to wound us or others.

Because the potential for good or evil in the healing ministry is so great, it is vital that our understanding of what constitutes proper faith for healing is properly founded. Not on what we have seen in a healing meeting, however dramatic it seemed, or on the words of any speaker, however impressive. Spirit-given discernment has to begin with an understanding of the place of faith in Jesus' own ministry of healing.

Faith in Jesus' ministry of healing

Faith which led to substantial risk-taking not only existed
in Jesus' ministry of healing: indeed it seemed to be
essential. Apparently though, the healings He ministered
depended not just on His faith, but on the simultaneous
presence of faith in others. However, three stories in
Matthew chapter 9 demonstrate that there was flexibility
over where the other faith could lie.

Firstly some men brought to Jesus a paralytic, lying on
a mat. It was when Jesus saw their faith that He said to
the paralytic 'Take heart, son; your sins are forgiven' (v2).
After a debate with the teachers of the law about whether
it was easier to say that sin was forgiven, or to say 'rise
up and walk', Jesus told the man to take his mat and
go home, which the man did. Though Jesus healed, it is
clear the faith of those who brought the man was vital.

Later in the chapter (vv20–22), Matthew relates the
story of the woman who had been bleeding for twelve
years. She touched the edge of Jesus' cloak, saying to
herself 'If I only touch his cloak, I will be healed'. Jesus
turned and saw her, saying 'Take heart, daughter, your
faith has healed you.' The woman was healed from that
moment. Later on (v27–30), Jesus healed two blind men
who had called out to Him 'Have mercy on us, Son of
David!' He asked them 'Do you believe that I am able to
do this?' When they replied 'Yes, Lord,' He touched their
eyes and said 'According to your faith will it be done to
you'. Their sight was immediately restored. In both these
cases, it was the faith of the ones who desired the healing
which was crucial.

Faith may also be centred in those ministering healing.
When Peter gave account of the healing of the lame man
in Acts 3 (the story of the man who asked for alms and
was given legs!) he emphasized it was not by personal
power or godliness, but 'by faith in the name of Jesus'.
He continued 'It is Jesus' name and the faith that comes
through him that has given this complete healing to him,

as you can all see' (v16). In this case it was the faith of Peter and John on which the healing pivoted.

Where faith was present, Jesus was even capable of healing at a distance, as the healing of the centurion's servant demonstrated (Matthew 8:5–13). Yet by contrast, a faithless atmosphere inhibited Him. When He was rejected by the people of Nazareth, due to their lack of faith which amazed Him 'He could not do any miracles there, except lay his hands on a few sick people and heal them' (Mark 6:5–6). Evidently, reciprocal faith in those being healed, or those surrounding the ones being healed was essential, even when it was Jesus who was directly ministering the healing.

The place of faith in healing was at the very core of Jesus' ministry of healing. What is at the core of our giving or receiving in the healing ministry is therefore critical to what happens. Great discernment is thus needed about the preaching and teaching of those who influence our faith for healing.

Faith in Anaheim

Anaheim, Los Angeles is not the only place in the world where there is faith for healing. However, it struck me during a visit there what a remarkable microcosm it presents of the leading influences that Christian people can be exposed to, whether we realize it or not.

The overriding cultural context of the Anaheim churches is secular faith in the American dream. Love it or hate it, Southern California is the quintessence of what hard work and a vision of building new things can bring about. It speaks of the endeavour to meet the unsatisfied cravings of the heart by getting more and more of the latest things. Here is to be found the original Disney Land, with its own faith in the potential of human nature to be happy. No alcohol, no sex, just good clean fun that can bless adults as well as children. Elizabeth Taylor's choice of it for her sixtieth birthday party 'for the child in her' endorses its power to enchant all who venture therein. If only for the length of a day ticket, it can heal a hurting heart.

A stone's-throw away in one direction, although not one it would be wise to throw one in, is the Crystal Cathedral. Its minister is Dr Robert Schuller, now to be seen on satellite television's *Hour of Power*. In this enormous edifice, built almost entirely of glass, is preached faith in a clean-cut religion that espouses American pragmatism. Here is the 'how to' approach. Seven ways to be an effective father. Ten steps to be a positive thinker. Five ways to make a church grow. Three steps to know God. For those who really don't want the exertion of getting out of their cars to go inside, but prefer the drive-in approach to church, huge glass doors open which allow the service to waft over them as they remain in the parking lot. Though not as extreme as the nearby drive-in church where they reputedly toot once for Amen and twice for Hallelujah, the style of such teaching makes faith accessible in a user-friendly way. Attractive as that is, it can become light, to say the least, on the mystery of faith.

In another direction, at the Anaheim Convention Center, none other than Kenneth Copeland was billed. His encouragement was to put faith in the prosperity gospel, which says that if we believe God aright, He will put special blessing on our efforts, and bring us into material abundance.

In the midst of this was the Anaheim Vineyard, humbly meeting in a converted warehouse, albeit of the proportions only Americans go for. Surrounded by some very different expressions of faith, John Wimber and his team have stuck as close as possible to their understanding of Jesus' ministry as the model of faith for healing. Their approach has provided a very effective datum from which to demonstrate that not all which glistens with faith and other phenomena may be gold. They have given a foil to the prevalent view that any expression of faith which results in something positive and tangible must have some authenticity.

Jesus warned (Luke 6:43,44) that the issue is not whether there is any fruit, but what is the root behind that fruit. Anaheim as a place demonstrates to us that wherever we are the need is to be circumspect about the root of faith even more than about the fruit of faith. In seeking to develop our understanding of the type of risky faith God is calling us to develop, particularly in the healing ministry, we need to be aware of the many influences that shape our perception of what we ought to be going for. We may indeed be very grateful for the contribution John Wimber has made. However, we need to be cautious about the far less helpful influences that may have come to us from Anaheim and elsewhere.

In particular, discernment is needed about the reflection of the pragmatic, 'how to' approach, which reckons that if something seems to work, it must be right. We may think we are more perceptive than the Californians, but many assume validation for a healing message if people are seen to fall over when they are prayed for. All that of itself validates is the reality of the supernatural.

Even more insidious is the influence of the Faith Movement's teaching on healing. Whilst its teaching on prosperity has largely been rejected in the United Kingdom, its influence on the broader understanding of healing has not been critiqued so clearly. It has apparently earthed healing in principles which look very scriptural, but as with prosperity teaching, it is only as they are tested that it becomes clear how much in the final analysis they veer away from biblical truth. Gutsy emphasis on faith looks very compelling, but does not automatically mean that it is the right sort of faith, in the right place. To this we will turn shortly.

Meanwhile, there is a conclusion we can draw for the more mature understanding of healing we are seeking. It needs a mature understanding of the place of faith. Yet, as we saw in the last chapter, such maturity does

not automatically mean we need the competence of a
theological giant to enter into it. To the contrary, what
may be far more necessary is the willingness to enter it
in simplicity. The key to it may well be to engage more
deeply with the significance of Jesus' words in Matthew
18:3: 'I tell you the truth, unless you change and become
like little children, you will never enter the kingdom of
heaven.'

The faith of children is remarkably uncomplicated. It
is neither about hype nor formula. Instead it is about
sincerity of heart, that continues to trust.

Certainly there are things we need to understand about
the place of faith within our lives and the three distinct
locations it should be found. Firstly, that of conversion
faith, which requires us to confess with our mouth 'Jesus
is Lord' (Romans 10:9). Secondly, that of continuing faith
which sustains us on the long-haul journey of being sure
of what we hope for and certain of what we do not see
(Hebrews 11:1). Thirdly, that of charismatic faith, which
is received as gift that is applied to specific circumstances
(1 Corinthians 12:9). However, discernment of the true
authenticity of each of these depends not on the pragmatic
criteria of this world, but on the criteria of the kingdom
of heaven. So it is with the place of faith in the ministry
of healing. We find it when we are willing to become as
little children.

7

What Sort Of Faith Is Needed For Healing?

One of the basic theses of the Faith Movement is that
God wants us well, right now. 'Healing is just as
much a part of the plan of redemption as salvation, the
Holy Spirit, and heaven as your eternal home. To stay
sick when Jesus has provided healing would be living far
below your privileges as a child of God,' writes Kenneth
Copeland.[1] In his view there is only one sort of faith
for healing. Before looking at the sort of faith a more
mature model of healing needs to reflect, we first need
to appreciate the dangers of the faith he proposes.

Kenneth Copeland argues that there are laws in the
spiritual realm which if applied properly, will bring
healing. 'Any time a believer has a problem receiving
healing, he usually suffers from ignorance of God's Word,
ignorance of his rights and privileges in Jesus Christ. To
fully understand your position, you need to realize what
took place many centuries ago between God and a man
named Abram'.[2]

He then outlines the nature of the Abrahamic Covenant,
to which God bound Himself, developing how Jesus' death
on the cross was to pay the full price of the redemption
offered under that covenant. Through this all the forces of
destruction which were brought with sin when it entered
the world would be done away with as they affected every
area of life: spiritual, mental, physical, financial and
social. Copeland continues by saying that 'Jesus bore
the curse of the Law. He bore every sickness and every
plague known to man. He bore pain and suffering. Why?

So that the blessing could come on us when we accept His sacrifice as our own. Because we are in Christ, we are Abraham's seed and heirs to the blessing.'[3] His argument is therefore that we have a covenant with God, and one of our covenant rights is the right to a healthy body.

How that right is secured is living by the principles of the Faith Movement. Positive confession is vital, and the expression 'making a quality decision to walk in divine health' is characteristic of what is involved. The King James translation of 2 Corinthians 4:13 is used to support this: 'We having the same spirit of faith, according as it is written, I believed, and therefore have I spoken; we also believe, and therefore speak.'

This means feelings, and indeed symptoms, may have to be denied. The kingdom is by implication totally here for believers, and it's entirely up to us how much we have of it. What is said is therefore vital. 'We possess what we confess' is one of the catch-phrases. However, the consequences of this approach can be dire.

In his illuminating critique of the Faith Movement, Dan McConnell in *The Promise of Health and Wealth* describes the consequences of refusing to seek medical care for illnesses.[4] Others have taken far more dangerous risks than I did with my eyesight, and have less happy endings to their stories. Though the Faith Movement may at face value make the rest of us look gutless, what McConnell goes on to show is the greatness of the danger to our spiritual as well as physical health that can come from pursuing it to its limits. He demonstrates how its origins can be traced back into the cultic connections of E.W. Kenyon with New Thought and Christian Science. These have then been interwoven with classical Pentecostalism and healing revivalism, making them appear authentic. For this reason, just as the prosperity gospel has been seen through, so the Faith Movement's approach to healing needs to be.[5] Unfortunately, its influence on the ministry of healing has been far more pervasive than is generally recognized. The reality is that it has probably been imbibed by many who don't even realize they've done so, let alone what lies behind it.

What needs to be appreciated is that underlying it is the implication that Christ died that we might inherit wealth, health, length of life and freedom from tribulation and hardship. This is the American dream in a Christian disguise. It is through nothing as overt as this however that most people become involved with it. The doorway is simply the acceptance of the view that just as there are laws in the physical realm which we may operate to our benefit, so there are in the spiritual realm. Having recognized faith as an essential ingredient in healing, the hunger to find out more is not surprising. So with sincere intent and without any aspiration for the American dream, it is possible to become involved with faith teaching. Unfortunately, the dangers in doing so can be far greater than are recognized.

When we enter into the realm of principles for the exercise of faith, we can be led to believe we can obligate the sovereign God to intervene as we declare He should. John and Paula Sandford speak uncompromisingly about the statement that if we apply faith, God must heal. They say that 'to try to make Him do anything is magic; magic is the operation of principles or laws of God to accomplish our own selfish ends. Even healing in this context is our own selfish end.'[6] They go on to speak of how teachers of the recent Faith Movement have unwittingly led many who are sincere Christians into what is effectively the operation of magic. They emphasize the need for corresponding repentance.

Faith in our words?

Another aspect of the Faith Movement concerns the power of confession, where our words have power to bring healing into being. An extract of a typical example of a recommended daily confession includes these words:

> I HAVE NEW POWER! I have power to tread on
> serpents and scorpions and over ALL THE POWER
> of the enemy AND NOTHING SHALL BY ANY
> MEANS HURT ME! I have power over all devils to
> cast them out! I can lay hands on the sick and they
> shall recover! I am more than a conqueror through
> Jesus Christ. I can do all things through Christ![7]

However unwittingly we do it, we in effect put ourselves
into the role of creator beings rather than created beings.
Not only this, but 'having what we say' can rapidly
become a selfishly oriented exercise. The consequence
of this is that faith can become 'faith in faith' rather
than faith in God. All this centres us on what we may
get out of the Covenant, rather than on the One who
gave the Covenant. The example of what happened to
the people of Israel when they allowed the Ark of the
Covenant rather than God Himself to become their focus
demonstrates the dangers involved.

The Ark of the Covenant contained the stone tablets of
the Covenant, a golden jar of manna from the wilderness
and Aaron's rod which budded. It also served as the
meeting place in the inner sanctuary of the tabernacle
where the Lord revealed His will to Moses, Aaron and
Joshua. The Ark was therefore the supreme symbol for
the people of Israel of the divine presence guiding His
people. It played a significant part in the crossing of
the Jordan and the fall of Jericho. Increasingly however,
the people of Israel used it like a charm, or a lucky
talisman, believing it would not only stave off evil, but
also guarantee victory in battle. Notwithstanding what it
symbolized and what it contained, both God's promise as
well as physical testimony that God acts supernaturally
to bring deliverance, He allowed it to be lost. The story
is told in 1 Samuel 4:1–11 of what happened to the
Israelites at Ebenezer at the hand of the Philistines.
God permitted a major defeat when the slaughter was
very great, and the Ark was lost.

The lesson is clear. We can have God's promise to heal and physical tokens of what He has done, which may be the symbol to us of His divine presence. What they must not be used for is as the guarantee that He has to act on our terms. Indeed when faith in the Covenant supersedes faith in God, we put ourselves in danger of at least short-term defeat and loss of what He has given, as He permits circumstances which might cause us to re-evaluate our spiritual position.

Why it is possible to be seduced by 'the message of faith' is that apparently significant things may be seen to happen in meetings where it is preached. Whilst God certainly can and does do very powerful things in people who are open to His touch, it must not automatically be assumed that the presence of 'spiritual phenomena' authenticate a message as being totally from God. McConnell's account of William Branham shows how astounding miracles could happen through one whose doctrine was marginal at best, and towards the end of his ministry became outright heretical.[8] It is the root, not the apparent fruit, of this teaching which needs exposing, and we must not be naive about our vulnerability to be deflected from the truth.

Paul's astonishment was that the Galatian church so quickly turned to a 'different gospel – which is no gospel at all' (Galatians 1:6–9). Why they were, as we can be, so easily led astray is not just fickleness. It is also because we have an enemy who delights in the use of subtle attractions, which seem remarkably like the real thing, to lure us in the wrong direction. It is for this reason that we are warned that: 'The coming of the lawless one will be in accordance with the work of Satan displaying all kinds of counterfeit miracles, signs and wonders' (2 Thessalonians 2:9). Satan knows our potential for fascination.

It seems remarkable to those of us born after World War II, that people would listen to the broadcast of counterfeit wartime newsreels by the enemy propagandist, Lord Haw-Haw. Yet they did. His strategy was to make his reports not only sound plausible, but even more illuminating than the genuine newsreels. Ultimately, through the interweaving of insidious lies into what seemed like truth, his aim was to break the morale of the British people. To return to the radio analogy used earlier, it is only to be expected that the devil will seek to transmit some broadcasts of healing which sound deceptively like the right thing. His goal will inevitably be to include sufficient attractive aspects within them, that will blind us to the destructiveness of the lies which have been included.

Great discernment is therefore needed about all teaching on healing, not just that which is obviously non-scriptural. The counterfeit will always have at least a measure of apparent credibility. It is therefore not surprising that at face value there is only a narrow dividing line between the valid exercise of a gift of faith for healing, and the exercise of the principles of faith for healing that the Faith Movement would propose.

An illustration of a God-given gift of faith for healing can be seen in the involvement of Jim Glennon in the healing of Julie Sheldon, described in *Dancer Off Her Feet*. She was in intensive care, crippled with dystonia, and her life was hanging in the balance. Jim Glennon exercised a specific gift of faith for healing, which he described as being on the basis of 'not doubting in his heart' based on Mark 11:20–26.[9] The dramatic improvement which followed his relatively brief prayer eventually led to her total recovery. One can only sympathize with the reaction of Julie's two daughters who said to her 'We prayed for you every night, and he only prayed for you once!' Yet it was evidently Jim Glennon's prayer of faith which was crucial for what happened. This was authentic faith, of the type which James wrote about; '. . . pray for each other so that you may be healed. The prayer of a righteous man is powerful and effective' (James 5:16).

Compare this with the type of faith that some, influenced by the Faith Movement, sought to urge upon David

Watson as he faced terminal illness. He described the difficulty he had with quite a few letters which said, 'Once you have claimed God's healing, you've got it!'[10] The distinction is the implied obligation of God to act because we have exercised faith. It takes no account of any understanding of the kingdom of God being both 'now and not yet', let alone of God's sovereignty. Prayer for healing ministered on the basis of a God-given gift of faith may appear very similar to that which emerges out of Faith Movement type praying. However it is the direction of the underlying roots which make all the difference as to, not only the fruit which it can yield, but also the appropriateness of the risk that it can call us into.

Faith through tribulation

Whilst the Faith Movement focuses on here-and-now healing as the divine right of every believer, John Wimber's teaching on power healing has very helpfully demonstrated how faith for healing primarily in the 'now' can still allow for the reality of the 'not yet'. However if we are to discover what constitutes a more mature model of healing, we need to recognize that Scripture also speaks about the sort of faith which is a counterpoint to this. Such faith allows for the possibility of healing in the 'now', but is primarily focused on the 'not yet'. We need to face the tough question posed by this. Just how are we to handle the intertwining in Scripture of such faith for God to primarily act in the 'not yet' with faith for God to primarily act in the here-and-now?

Perhaps the best example of this is the classic discourse on faith in Hebrews chapter 11. One instance after another is given of the great exploits of those who did things 'by faith'. Abel, Enoch, Noah, Abraham, Isaac, Jacob, Joseph, Moses' parents, Moses and Rahab who are all cited for their faith, on the one hand saw God do extraordinary things as they kept faith in Him, yet on the other hand: 'They did not receive the things promised;

they only saw them and welcomed them from a distance'
(v13). 'Instead, they were longing for a better country –
a heavenly one' (v16).

Though this pre-dates the 'now and not yet' of the
kingdom which Jesus inaugurated, it fits with the 'now
and not yet' experience of God's action in our lives as
members of His kingdom. His supernatural intervention
in this world resulted in difficult circumstances being
overcome for these Old Testament saints, yet it could
not be described as the fulfilment of all that they were
believing for.

Time prohibited the writer to go on to describe all he
wanted to about Gideon, Barak, Samson and the prophets
who by faith:

> . . . conquered kingdoms, administered justice, and
> gained what was promised; who shut the mouths of
> lions, quenched the fury of the flames, and escaped
> the edge of the sword; whose weakness was turned
> to strength; and who became powerful in battle and
> routed foreign armies. Women received back their
> dead, raised to life again . . .
>
> (vv32–35a)

Suddenly though, in mid-verse, the whole emphasis of
the out-working of faith changes from the experience of
triumph, albeit in the context of 'now and not yet', into
the experience of tribulation.

> Others were tortured and refused to be released, so
> that they might gain a better resurrection. Some
> faced jeers and flogging, while still others were
> chained and put in prison. They were stoned; they
> were sawn in two; they were put to death by the
> sword. They went about in sheepskins and goatskins,
> destitute, persecuted and ill-treated – the world was
> not worthy of them. They wandered in deserts and
> mountains, and in caves and holes in the ground.
>
> (vv35b–38)

However, in no sense is the latter experience of faith seen as less than that of the previous group, for the passage concludes: 'These were all commended for their faith, yet none of them received what had been promised.' (v39).

Hebrews chapter 11, therefore, speaks of faith being equally God-honouring when the outworking of it has no immediate triumph in the 'now', but which looks only for God's triumph to be manifest in the 'not yet'. That 'not yet' may still be in this world but could be beyond the perceived time-scale of the believer or beyond the orbit perceived by the believer for how others may be touched by their witness of faith. Alternatively, it may be in eternity as the spiritual realm witnesses the testimony of the martyrs who overcame by the blood of the Lamb and the word of their testimony (Revelation 12:11). Indeed the picture of the martyrs (Revelation 6:9–11) calling out to God to avenge their blood, and being told to wait until the number of their brothers who were similarly to be killed was completed, takes it even further. It suggests that this model is not just God-honouring, but can actually be God-ordained.

This same understanding of faith was demonstrated by Shadrach, Meshach and Abednego in their reply to Nebuchadnezzar. When he threatened them with the fiery furnace because of their refusal to worship the image of gold he had set up they answered:

'O Nebuchadnezzar, we do not need to defend our-selves before you in this matter. If we are thrown into the blazing furnace, the God we serve is able to save us from it, and he will rescue us from your hand, O king. But even if he does not, we want you to know, O king, that we will not serve your gods or worship the image of gold you have set up.'

(Daniel 3:16–18)

These were mighty words of faith, believing for God's intervention, but whether the triumph was to be in the 'now' or the 'not yet' they left to God. In their case, God intervened in a dramatic way through the appearance of a fourth man walking in the fire who appeared to Nebuchadnezzar like a son of the gods. It was not long before Nebuchadnezzar approached the opening of the furnace, honouring them as servants of the Most High God, and calling them to come out. This they did, totally unharmed, without even the smell of smoke on them. The faith risk they took was not centred on a positive confession that God would save them, only a conviction that He could. They acknowledged it was in His hands.

The supreme example of this balance of faith is inevitably to be found in Jesus. He had the power to know supernatural deliverance, such as He demonstrated at Nazareth. After the people there rejected Him, they led Him to the brow of a hill to throw Him down the cliff. They failed. 'He walked right through the crowd, and went on his way' (Luke 4:30). However, He resolutely chose to go the way of the cross, setting His face to go to Jerusalem, knowing it would lead to crucifixion. Even in the face of being tempted to come down from the cross, because that would be the ultimate wonder which would cause others to believe, He chose to exercise faith to go the way of tribulation, looking to the 'not yet' of healing rather than the 'now'.

Jesus was to be glorified through His triumph over the powers and authorities on the cross (Colossians 2:15). Yet it was only because of His faith to go into the eye of the ultimate storm of tribulation that this happened. Though Jesus made the one sacrifice needed for all, we need to remember He also said: 'Whoever serves me must follow me; and where I am, my servant also will be' (John 12:26).

It is a far more attractive proposition to understand faith as that which enables us to circumnavigate the storm, than to go through it. Once helping to crew a

racing yacht across the English Channel, I was greatly
excited to discover the potential of the boat to slide around
a storm. What I didn't experience was its ability to go
right through the eye of the storm – providing, that is,
the crew has the sea-legs for it, which I suspect I hadn't!
Faith in God is sufficient for going through the eye of
the severest storm if we have the spiritual sea-legs it
needs. Human nature being what it is, our preference
is to go around the storm. Jesus' message of faith was
neither to do with comfort nor convenience. Its primary
focus was that we might follow Him on a faith journey
which goes the very opposite way human inclination
would take us.

This manifestly needs to be reflected in a more mature
model of healing. Scripture has put alongside the power
healing model, with its encouragement to develop faith
for what God can do now, this other sort of faith for
healing, which sees its outworking in the 'not yet'. It
suggests a very different understanding of God's leading
us in triumphal procession in Christ (2 Corinthians
2:14) to the superficial triumphalism that is sometimes
preached. In fact it potentially calls for a far higher level
of faith and risk. Yet it is properly founded risk. It trusts
all to the God who promises never to fail or forsake those
whose desire is not for their own benefit, but for the glory
of God, be it in the 'now' or the 'not yet', whichever He
should choose.

The need for such an understanding of healing is
essential if the ministry of it is not to be seduced in
one way or another by the devil. As Adrian Chatfield
wrote in *Anglicans For Renewal*

Any theology of signs and power which leaves out
the cross becomes demonic in its triumphalism; con-
versely, any theology which omits this continuing
powerful activity of God becomes demonic in its fatal-
ism. A genuine proclamation of the gospel requires
both poles to be preached in equal measure, except

where the balance has to be corrected because of earlier omissions.[11]

Perhaps it was this that my eyes were most opened to through my encounter with the Faith Movement's approach to healing!

Are There Limits To What God Will Heal?

Horizons are strange things. Though they don't physically exist, they still define the limits of what you
can physically see. Yet, they also depend on your vantage point. The higher you go, the broader the horizon
becomes, and the further you can see. Apparently this is
how it is in the ministry of healing. The power healing
model has lifted our sights. In doing so, it has extended
our vision of where the limits of the healing we can
minister might lie. So it is tempting to conclude that
to push those limits out further still, we need to keep
climbing the mountain of power healing. Our goal in the
healing ministry could well seem to be that of the Alpine
mountaineer whose epitaph read 'He died climbing'.

Certainly, to develop a more mature understanding of
healing, we need to do whatever it takes to broaden our
horizons. Whether that would be achieved by continually
seeking to scale new heights is, however, another question.
Not only my personal experience, but also that of others
whom I increasingly began to observe, suggested that it
may be rather more complex than that. We seemed to be
running up against limitations. Could it actually be, I wondered, that there are upper limits on what God will heal?

At first sight it seems incompatible with God's nature
that there should be limits. He is the God of limitless
compassion. 'The Lord is gracious and compassionate,
slow to anger and rich in love. The Lord is good to
all; he has compassion on all he has made' (Psalm
145:8–9). Jesus' parable of the lost son pictures the

father, seeing his returning son while still far off, being filled with compassion (Luke 15:20). It speaks of God's heart towards all who return to Him, humbly seeking restoration. Jesus had compassion on the crowds, because they were harassed and helpless, 'like sheep without a shepherd' (Matthew 9:36). The word used there is very powerful, meaning 'to have the bowels yearning'. Jesus healed out of compassion. His heart went out to the widow of Nain, whose only son had died (Luke 7:13), to blind men crying out to him by the roadside (Matthew 20:34) and to a leper begging to be made clean (Mark 1:41). We too are to reflect the compassion of God towards one another (1 Peter 3:8).

However, the greater one's perception of the compassion of God, the harder it is to handle the tough questions raised when healing does not come. Unless, that is, we recognize that compassion is only one of the basic attributes of God. Scripture also teaches that God is sovereign, and as such, He is not obligated to dispense compassion on demand. This may create mystery for us, with our limited horizons of understanding, particularly as to why He may seem to bless one but not another. But if it does, we will not be the first to struggle with it.

Paul uses the story of Rebekah's children to illustrate that such mystery is not a new experience. They had the same father, Isaac, 'yet, before the twins were born or had done anything good or bad – in order that God's purpose in election might stand: not by works but by him who calls – she was told, "The older will serve the younger"'. Paul counters the response that this means God is unjust. He quotes God's words when Moses asked to see His glory 'I will have mercy on whom I have mercy, and I will have compassion on whom I have compassion' (Romans 9:10–15).

Paul is saying that God does not owe mercy and compassion to anyone. It is because of His grace alone that we receive anything. Our experiences of lack of healing may bewilder us. Some may be due to reasons in us rather than in God. Others may only be explained by understanding that alongside God's compassion in healing must be put His sovereignty.

It is therefore a false assumption that we can categorize healing into a series of propositions and practices that we expect God to conform to. We may certainly anticipate God moving through us with increasing power if we seek Him wholeheartedly. This does not mean, however, that if for our part we can 'get it right', healing must increasingly happen to order. Such thinking misunderstands God's ways of working, and the sovereignty of His timing.

God's sovereignty in healing

The disciples themselves, seeing the risen Lord, were tempted to this view. Their question 'Lord, are you at this time going to restore the kingdom to Israel?' (Acts 1:6) was very reasonable. Had we been with them doubtless we also would have concluded that, with enough faithful endeavour, it needn't be too long before all disease and sickness would be eliminated, and even Israel restored to its proper relationship with God. However, it was a vision Jesus soon quashed. The relevance of His response was to go far beyond those disciples, to all who are looking for the development of healing models which anticipate increasing effectiveness.

'It is not for you to know the times or dates the Father has set by his own authority' Jesus replied (v7). God is sovereign, and the reconciliation of all things will happen only when He declares it will be. Douglas McBain has pointed out that the error the disciples had fallen into can be described as 'over-realized eschatology'.[1] They were wanting to see more of the presence of the future than it was God's will and purpose to reveal at that time. Despite the rightness of hungering for it, they also needed to accept the sovereign purposes of God. He is both totally full of compassion, and also totally sovereign regarding

the outworking of His compassion. The disciples' remit
was to exercise to the full their experience of the Spirit,
but also to accept the greater context of God's sovereign
purposes. In effect, to accept limitations on what they
would see of the kingdom of God in their time.

The question this poses for us is whether the present
day rediscovery of the healing ministry has led us into an
error similar to that of the disciples. Certainly the power
healing model has taken us to new heights of expectancy
about the possibilities for the kingdom of God to break in.
We have seen practical demonstration that the healings
which Jesus ministered were signs of it. These signs the
church was both authorized and empowered to continue,
not just at the beginning, but for its entire history. We
have been shown that the age of miracles has not ceased,
and that our lack of experience of healing points not to the
abnormality of the early church, but to the abnormality of
our own experience and worldview.

Just as the early church experienced substantial growth,
so we have been encouraged to believe that we may
expect to as well, if we will move into an appropriate
faith, with corresponding risk-taking. John Wimber and
others have personally shown that the Holy Spirit may
be depended on to honour such steps, and to confirm our
faith with His supernatural interventions, resulting not
just in healings, but in evangelistic effectiveness. Some
very wide-ranging renewal of the church has already
followed from it.

So it can be tempting to wonder whether there is any
upper limit to it, if we can just 'get it right'. However, the danger comes when such teaching is accepted
unquestioningly. Alfred Korzybski said that 'there are
two ways we can slide through life easily: to believe
everything or to doubt everything; both ways save us
from thinking'. In the light of 'over-realized eschatology',
rather than just seeking new ways to climb higher in the
healing ministry to get past our present limitations, perhaps we need to think about whether God has permitted

them for a reason. Indeed what He might be saying through them.

Firstly, God may be speaking of the danger of the gospel message of healing becoming focused on signs, wonders and other phenomena. Ultimately, the greatest healing that the gospel ministers is salvation from sin. It is received through the power of forgiveness centred on what Christ alone accomplished on the cross. It is not through signs, wonders and phenomena, however dramatic they are. Such was the point Jesus sought to make to the Pharisees and teachers of the law when he forgave the sins of the paralytic who was lowered through the roof, before healing him physically (Luke 5:17–26). There and then, the biggest need of the man would have seemed to be able to walk. Having now had almost two thousand years in Paradise, though doubtless still grateful that Jesus healed his legs, what he will be vastly more grateful for is the fact that Jesus forgave his sins.

Though physical healing may not be for all, God's unfailing compassion means that absolute forgiveness is unreservedly available for all who desire to receive it. In the light of eternity, this is an infinitely more important healing than anything bodies ever receive in this world. The rediscovery of healing which is tangible and dramatic must never be allowed to mask this truth.

Secondly, God may be speaking of the danger of focusing healing primarily on our own needs. For Jesus to minister healing to the poor, the disadvantaged and the marginalized of society was a very powerful sign. Not only did it mean physical restoration of their bodies, it meant restoration to a society from which they had become outcasts. Though understandable to want God to heal us miraculously when we are incapacitated, it is a rather different sign we are seeking to that which Jesus ministered. If we desire to see the compassion of God most powerfully expressed through the healing ministry, it is more probable we will see it if we go out to the poor and needy of our day. Perhaps even more likely if we forego some of our own opportunities for healing in doing so. It is as we look outwards towards the needs of an unhealed world, rather than inwards towards our own ailments, that the world is more likely to take notice. This is most of all what God's heart is for.

Thirdly, God may be speaking of the danger that we conclude there is one methodology of healing, in which the right words and the right presence of healing power will make it happen. Though there are headline stories of physical healings, the track record suggests they are not quite so common as we would like to think. In fact physical healing of an obviously miraculous kind is not particularly common. We have already considered why miracles are in any case for God the 'road less travelled', to use the phrase of Nigel Wright.[2] Honesty also compels us to conclude that if there is one methodology for healing to be found, no one has yet discovered it! For those whose desire is to co-operate with God's sovereign purposes of bringing healing to this world, it will require more insight than any one methodology can bring.

What a more mature model of healing therefore needs to embrace is the reality of those limitations God may permit regarding how far healing may be experienced. They may be because there is a specific word He wants the church to become open to. They may also be because of His sovereign purposes of which we have no comprehension, particularly in relation to His timing. It is certainly possible to see seasons of healing in church history that point to God's sovereignty. Furthermore, in Jesus' own ministry, the comment is made on one occasion that 'the power of the Lord was present for him to heal the sick' (Luke 5:17). The reasons for more favourable and less favourable seasons for healing may be difficult to appreciate from our perspective. What is clear however is that we cannot broaden the horizons of healing simply by our own efforts to climb higher.

However, this begs another question. Given the way kingdom principles often work the opposite way to those of this world, is there a horizon of healing that can be opened out for us, perhaps even a limitless one, by moving in our understanding of healing in some other direction than ever upwards?

The greater purpose of healing

Scripture defines spiritual maturity as 'attaining to the whole measure of the fullness of Christ' (Ephesians 4:13). The greatest loss at the Fall was not our physical health, or our psychological well-being, but our capacity to glorify God: to be able to say 'Your will, not mine'. The ultimate healing from God is thus to conform us 'to the likeness of his Son, that he might be the first born among many brothers' (Romans 8:29).

To have a body which has been healed is a blessing. However, to have a heart which is not just forgiven, but is increasingly being made into the likeness of the heart of God is an even greater gift of wholeness. There are no indications anywhere that God limits the amount of healing He will give to those who truly want to be made more like Jesus, through living as His disciples. The acid test of the extent to which we really want this is in how we want God to transform our experience of disease. Do we just want Him to take the 'dis' out of 'disease' to leave us with 'ease', or do we want Him to change 'disease' into 'discipleship', which may not offer completely abundant ease to us?

What this choice is about is exemplified by the two archetypes of New Testament discipleship, Peter and Paul. Through them notable healings were ministered. Yet both experienced physical incapacitation and suffering, as God in His compassion and sovereignty used them as channels of His greater healing purposes to a fallen world.

Peter's experience of God on the 'road less travelled' was very real. His reputation for healing was such that people brought the sick into the streets and laid them on mats that at least his shadow might fall on some of them as he passed by (Acts 5:15). He also experienced a miraculous release from prison (Acts 12:3–10). If anyone should have been able to live in fullness of health to the end of their days, he should have. Though it cannot be proved that he was crucified in Rome, he knew even before all these momentous events that he was not going to have an easy end to his days.

This he had learnt after the breakfast on the beach which he and the other disciples had had with the resurrected Jesus. Three times Jesus had asked Peter if he loved Him, ministering healing to his woundedness of spirit caused by his three denials of Jesus before the fire in the high priest's courtyard. Now he was in the fire of refinement. Soon he was to be on fire with the Spirit. The end of that journey for him, however, was not to be in a blaze of glory like Elijah going up in the chariot of fire.

'When you were younger,' Jesus said, 'you dressed yourself and went where you wanted; but when you are old you will stretch out your hands, and someone else will dress you and lead you where you do not want to go.' John comments that Jesus said this to indicate the kind of death by which Peter would glorify God. Then Jesus said to him 'Follow me!' (John 21: 18,19). The outworking of that glory Peter would not see on earth. For him it was to be in the 'not yet'. It would involve the need to stay the course of discipleship, and would not be an increasing experience of ease.

Given that Peter was the rock on which the church would be built, this suggests his experience was characteristic of what all disciples would experience. It points to the possibility of occasional miracles, to the ministering of healing which may even be dramatic and to healing that brings ease to our inner selves. However, it also points to the need for a willingness to face tribulation for the sake of the Lord, which may go as far as martyrdom. Miracles will not always be there to get us out of difficult situations. It is through this style of discipleship that God desires to minister healing to a broken world.

Paul's experience further endorses it. He was also used for dramatic healings. At Ephesus God did such extraordinary things through him that even handkerchiefs and aprons that had touched him were taken to the sick. Their illnesses were cured and evil spirits left them (Acts 19:11–12). He had evidently undergone substantial inner healing to be able to say that 'to live is Christ and to die is gain' (Philippians 1:21). He was at ease within himself, yet his circumstances were anything but easy. He endured great difficulties in his missionary tours taking him almost to the point of death and finally to the incapacitation of imprisonment. Yet through his discipleship, the good news of God's healing purposes for a broken world was broadcast very far and wide.

Realistic expectations for healing

The stories of Peter and Paul demonstrate what is involved in the change of orientation from self-concern to concern for God and others. It is the reversal of that bending of our orientation which took place in Eden. The process should not be underestimated. If Christ Himself learned obedience from what He suffered (Hebrews 5:8) and we are to enter into the fellowship of sharing in his sufferings (Philippians 3:10) then the journey into that maturity is not going to be a journey of ease.

Realistic expectation is for that journey primarily to be about the experience of discipleship through difficulty. It is not God's miraculous interventions themselves which will change our hearts, however much they might amaze us. The truest healing of our being will happen in the circumstances He permits us to encounter. Some we may be allowed to overcome triumphantly, but others we will be left to learn through.

This is not to deny the place of either power healing, or what might be called pastoral healing. The mandate for pastoral healing in Scripture is clear. When sickness is encountered, the elders of the church should be called for, to pray, and to anoint with oil in the name of the Lord (James 5:14). Where lack of health is impeding God's purposes, authority is given to pray in faith that the sick person will be made well. When suffering, there is the basis of God's compassion from which to pray. The answer may not always come through prayer alone. Paul in fact encouraged Timothy to 'stop drinking only water, and use a little wine because of your stomach and your frequent illnesses' (1 Timothy 5:23). Discernment is therefore needed to distinguish between that which God simply wants to put right that we might get on with life, which may be expedited remarkably quickly, and that in which He may have some deeper purpose.

In power healing, John Wimber has shown us the reality of the mountain tops of healing. It may be the 'road less travelled' for God, but He does indeed travel it. For those who are able to scale the heights involved, the view can indeed be spectacular. However, as John Wimber points out, the scriptural evidence suggests that the healing of the chronically sick is far more probable, if not mostly limited to, evangelistic settings.[3] These healings vindicate the preaching of the gospel and are demonstrations of God's power.

Power healing is therefore to be sought as a part of the equipping God gives, that people's intellectual doubts about Him might be superseded by a tangible experience of His touch. He also wants to enliven our faith for the reality of His kingdom through it. Yet, as the incident with Simon the sorcerer teaches, recorded in Acts 8:18–21, it requires rightness of heart on our part to receive it. It is not acquired cheaply. Furthermore, we are not to so model our total theology around it that we like the first disciples, also fall into the error of 'over-realized eschatology'. The fact is that even those who benefit from power healing are still called to journey forwards in discipleship, with all that the outworking of that will mean in their lives.

To climb the spectacular mountain-tops of power healing is as with all mountaineering. Though increasing numbers are succeeding at it, not everyone is able to do it. Even those who can are unable to stay on the top indefinitely, as was demonstrated by the thirty eight people who in May 1993 reached the top of Everest on the same day. What was a pioneering achievement for Sir Edmund Hillary and Sherpa Tenzing in 1953 is now accessible to many, but still only on a purely limited basis. So too with what John Wimber has pioneered in making power healing accessible. We owe a great debt to him, but we also need to recognize the limitations of what he has opened up. Perhaps most importantly, we need to also recognize the direction we can go where there are far less limitations on the healing we may minister and receive. Far from being found in getting higher up the mountain, it is found in venturing forth in another direction altogether.

Going through the valley

Valleys, from which there is no spectacular view, feel like places of vulnerability and weakness. To our way of thinking they are uncomfortable places to be. Yet if we are willing to co-operate with God in them, they can be the place of mighty opportunity, as the story of the defeat of the Arameans by the people of Israel in 1 Kings 20:23–30 describes.

The Israelites were good hand-to-hand fighters and had been successful against their enemies in the hill country, but they were no match for their enemies' chariots of iron in the plains. Following a severe defeat in the hills, the Arameans concluded that 'Their gods are gods of the hills. That is why they were too strong for us. But if we fight them on the plains, surely we will be stronger than they'. Yet the Israelites did choose to march out and face the

Arameans in the plain. They were 'like two small flocks
of goats, while the Arameans covered the countryside'.
However, a man of God told the king of Israel 'This is
what the Lord says: "Because the Arameans think the
Lord is a god of the hills and not a god of the valleys, I
will deliver this vast army into your hands, and you will
know that I am the Lord".'

For seven days they camped opposite each other. It
was a protracted time for the Israelites to keep their
nerve. Then battle was joined. The Israelites inflicted
one hundred thousand casualties on the Arameans in a
single day. The rest escaped to the city of Aphek, where
a wall collapsed on a further twenty-seven thousand of
them.

Choosing to fight in the place of vulnerability resulted
in even greater glory being given to God. So it is with
the healing ministry. Our preference is bound to be for
healings which are immediate and physically demon-
strable. Yet even greater opportunity lies in positively
doing battle in the place in which there are no easy
answers. We do so in faith that God is able to work
through situations which may seem bad in themselves.
That He has purposes in both the 'not yet' as well as the
now, which we may not be able to see, but which we look
to in faith, confident of His limitless power to bring good
out of evil.

Going into the valley may be unavoidable for us,
through the normal flow of life, or as a particular consequence of our discipleship. It is still our choice as to what
we do when we find ourselves there. Whether we face the
enemy, or apply our energies to avoiding the battle in that
situation of vulnerability. However, without victory there
as well, the implication is that God is only the Lord our
Healer on the mountains, but not in the valleys. If the
heart of the disciple is for the greatest glory to be given
to God, there is only one option.

This involves the willingness to be as those two small
flocks of goats against a vast army. There may even be a

protracted time of waiting in which nerve has to be kept. Yet, as David was to write in Psalm 23, 'Even though I walk through the valley of the shadow of death, I will fear no evil, for you are with me; your rod and your staff, they comfort me'. When as disciples we venture forwards in the valley, we venture further into both the maturity and the mystery of faith, which is Christ in us, the hope of glory (Colossians 1:27). The potential of such healing is limitless.

When Is Deliverance The Only Answer?

Phone calls on my day off are one thing Françoise tries to keep from me. This one was different. It was from a young lady who urgently needed help. Some months earlier she had informed me how God had told her to leave our congregation to join a small para-church grouping. She was adamant about it, and there was no opportunity to discuss with her what she might be getting herself into. All I could do was pray the Lord's blessing on her as she went. In parting, I had said that if ever she needed to, she was still welcome to contact me.

Over the phone, she related how the day before members of the group she had joined had delivered her from twenty different spirits. Far from this bringing peace, it had left her in turmoil. 'Have I been that severely possessed by the devil?' she kept asking. 'Didn't Mary Magdalene only have seven . . .' From what I knew of her, it seemed unlikely that she had been possessed by even one demon. I could understand how the ministry she had been subjected to had left her traumatized.

When we met, I managed to minister a degree of peace to her by showing how the word 'spirit' is used several different ways in Scripture. Certainly, it can refer to a demonic, possessing presence in a person. Equally, it can simply refer to an attitude or emotion, which in no sense is about the literal presence of a demon. Through looking at this together, some of the confusion that had been put on her was resolved. Yet the 'demonomania' had hurt her badly and the whole experience was likely to leave some permanent scars. What was more, through what had been done to her, she had been diverted from receiving the healing the Lord could have worked in her. Her confidence in the healing ministry would take a long while to rebuild.

Driving back afterwards, I reflected on the good and the bad which has come about from the deliverance ministry. For the very small percentage of instances where it is actually what is needed, it has been immensely beneficial. The exposure of the devil's capacity to put demonic hold on people, and the rediscovery of the power to deliver people from it, has resulted in unimaginable breakthrough for some. Yet the devil has retaliated. He has done this by deluding a far greater number that it is through this form of ministry they will receive the healing they need. It is a clever deception. Not only are they on a spiritual wild-goose chase looking for healing in a place where, for them, it is not to be found, they are also diverted from the process and the depth of healing that God would truly desire to minister to them. The tough question of how to know when deliverance ministry is appropriate is certainly part of the agenda for a more mature model of healing. It is one the devil in his rearguard action has managed to cause much confusion over.

It struck me how the devil's pattern of retaliation is similar to that of Saddam Hussein when he was evicted from Kuwait. It was a mighty conquest to see the domination of such an aggressor brought to an end so decisively. Yet though he was a defeated foe, he left behind the carnage of hundreds of fiercely blazing oil wells. Each one was an inferno that desecrated the newly liberated territory. Not only did they cause terrible destruction, but also a distraction of gigantic proportions that was to preoccupy the liberators as well as the Kuwaitis for a good while after the land was freed.

Similarly, as the devil has been forced to retreat from ground he has held in people's lives, he has left behind his own fires. His strategy has also been to cause both destruction and distraction. Destruction which seeks to diminish the worth to its rightful owners of the spiritual ground that has been liberated. Distraction to prevent the liberators from focusing on where he still holds power and where the battle needs to be taken on into. The devil knows how even a suspicion of fire grabs attention and diverts people from what they should otherwise be about. For greater victory to be achieved, let alone sustained, in the ministry of healing, the devil's strategy needs exposing for what it is.

Exposing the strategy of destruction

The most obvious aspect of the destruction the devil would seek to inflict is on innocent victims such as in the story just related. Misplaced suspicion that demonic smoke could be smelt was enough not only to let off the fire-alarm but to set in motion the drama of a full call-out. Such false call-outs only play into the devil's hands. They can destroy a great measure of confidence in the liberation that Christ has made available. The assurance that 'if the Son sets you free, you will be free indeed' (John 8:36) can be greatly undermined.

However, it is not just the individuals themselves whose spiritual conviction regarding the victory of Jesus can be eroded. The Allies who physically liberated Kuwait were also affected by Saddam's scorched earth policy. Indeed, not only they, but all who watched were left questioning at the time how much of a victory it really was to win back a land which looked so damaged by what the enemy had done to it. So it can be not only for those directly involved in the healing ministry, but also for those who observe it. The publicity generated by any undue attention to the demonic realm is destructive to more than just those directly involved. It impinges beyond the greater Christian community on to its witness about the degree of victory that has been secured over the realm of evil.

Saddam Hussein was aware that propaganda had a role to play in his battle. The more fear he could induce about his potential for destruction through the fires he might light, the more this might cause people to see his retreat as something less than total defeat. He saw the potential power there was in conjuring up fear, however exaggerated it was. It is not hard to see where he derived such thinking from. As Nigel Wright has written in *The Fair Face of Evil* 'When demons or the devil get undue attention from Christians they welcome it. It is a way in which they themselves are boosted. It is a form of energy which they absorb into themselves and which enables them to go on feeding off the human energy from which they exist.'[1] His point is that the power of darkness actually grows and increases to the extent to which 'faith' is given to it.

Even in legitimate deliverance ministry, the devil's rearguard strategy of destruction still needs watching. To the seventy-two who returned rejoicing that the demons submitted to them in the Lord's name, Jesus issued a warning. 'Do not rejoice that the spirits submit to you, but rejoice that your names are written in heaven' (Luke 10:20). However successful deliverance ministry may be, if the focus ends up on demons rather than on heaven, the devil has left at least the smell of demonic smoke.

The devil's strategy of retaliatory destruction in the face of an effective ministry of healing, in order to suggest he hasn't lost completely, needs exposing. However, that is not his only strategy. His other is to distract from what he is still doing and where he still has hold which hasn't yet been noticed. Distraction is, by its very nature, a far more subtle strategy than overt attempts to cause retaliatory destruction. It is, at least potentially, also far more dangerous.

Exposing the strategy of distraction

Deliverance ministry can itself become a distraction. Though it might be dramatic and command much attention, it is not an end in itself. Scripture overall does not say that much about it. Indeed, the New Testament treats it as only incidental to what really matters, which is the bringing in of the kingdom of God. Ministry that requires the hierarchies of demons to be understood in order to effect deliverance can therefore lead into a most tenuous use of Scripture. It can all too easily offer the devil opportunity to deflect those who would pursue it from the central thrust of Scripture.

There is much we would like to know about how the evil realm operates. However, the construction of Scripture suggests that for our own good, neither should we, nor may we. Otherwise we would fall prey even more easily to being distracted from the things which really matter.

The greatest is the scale of the victory Jesus has won, and the fact of His omnipresence. The more we appreciate it, the more it exposes the limitation of the devil's power, and of his inability to be omnipresent. The discovery of the apparent existence of so many demons, whether false or true, can only serve to fuel the devil's fire. It can so easily be taken to be far greater than it is. If this happens, he has succeeded in distracting us from the true balance of things.

A smashed car windscreen is an effective analogy for how this can come about. The cracks go everywhere, suggesting that the whole windscreen has been hit. It looks as if something enormous must have hit it for the damage to be all over. However, the truth is that the point of impact would have been very localized, and all the resultant crazing of the glass is purely secondary. The devil wants to lure us into the equivalent of looking at every broken fragment of life we can find, in order to draw the assumption that each piece has been individually hit. If we do this, he knows he can draw us into totally false conclusions about his presence and his power.

The utterly disproportionate emphasis there is on demons as compared with angels demonstrates our potential for distraction from the truth which really matters. If we understand the potential of demons as fallen angels to harm, why do we not have even greater perception of the power of angels to do good? The reason why in the mid-seventies Billy Graham wrote *Angels: God's Secret Agents* was because of the minimal literature he could find on the subject, compared with shelves full of books on demons, the occult and the devil. He quotes John Calvin who, in Volume 1 of his *Institutes of the Christian Religion*, wrote 'Angels are the dispensers and administrators of the divine beneficence toward us. They regard our safety, undertake our defence, direct our ways, and exercise a constant solicitude that no evil befall us.'

Billy Graham goes on to say 'Angels have a much more important place in the Bible than the devil and his demons. Therefore, I undertook a biblical study of the subject of angels. Not only has it been one of the most fascinating studies of my life, but I believe the subject is more relevant today than perhaps at any time in history.'[2]

Since he wrote those words, both their relevance and the interest in the demonic has become, if anything, even greater, yet the understanding of angels is no more prominent now than then. Given the increased awareness of the deliverance ministry since then, there can be only one conclusion. In the face of defeat over the rediscovery of the deliverance ministry, the devil has been working a strategy to minimize his losses. That strategy is to cause retaliatory destruction wherever he can. Furthermore, to harness the opportunity of the battle to distract away from what he is still doing and which has yet to be confronted.

If this is true for healing that arises from the deliverance ministry, then there is no reason why it is not his strategy in relation to the total sweep of the healing ministry. How he goes about it is what needs exposing.

Seeing through the devil's smoke screen

The fires lit by Saddam Hussein in Kuwait not only caused destruction and distraction, but also caused what must have been the greatest smoke screen of history. In old-fashioned warfare, it would have given him enormous opportunity for counter-manoeuvre. However, the Allies had the technology to see what the human eye could not. They were able to look beyond the smoke screen, to identify exactly what power the enemy still had, and where it was placed. Consequently, they were able to complete his expulsion from the occupied territory.

The devil's strategy from the start has been deception, always seeking to manoeuvre behind whatever smoke screens he may find. Given the battleground that the healing ministry is, it would be naive to think that human eyesight alone can see through the smoke screen the devil is currently hiding behind. By ourselves we are not able to perceive the ground he still holds, be it in society, within churches or in us as individuals. Nor can we with human eyesight perceive the manoeuvres he is seeking to make in relation to us.

The promise of Scripture however is that 'the one who is in you is greater than the one who is in the world' (1 John 4:4). This means that in Jesus, we can see through the smoke screen the devil would seek to hide behind. However, to receive the eyesight Jesus alone can give requires the humble acknowledgement of our blindness, and the specific request for His gift of sight.

When Jesus called the obviously blind Bartimaeus to Him, He asked what seems like a most surprising question. 'What do you want me to do for you?' Jesus was not however just inviting Bartimaeus to own the seriousness of his blindness. He was inviting Him to express specific faith that Jesus could heal it. Bartimaeus replied 'Rabbi,

I want to see' (Mark 10:51). We too need to say the same to Jesus if we are to get spiritual vision through the devil's smoke screen.

For it to mean anything, there has first to be some revelation of the degree of our blindness. Be it in relation to the need of healing in society, or in particular churches, or in individuals we are in the process of ministering to. Before we can properly say what we want Jesus to do for our spiritual sight, we need to appreciate how blind we are to the ground the devil still holds against healing, let alone to the counter-manoeuvres he may be making even at this moment.

The extent to which the devil's beguiling power can operate imperceptibly is not to be underestimated. He has the capacity to delude an entire nation. An illuminating example of this is given by Francis Schaeffer in *The Great Evangelical Disaster*. He refers to the parallel between the arguments used in America to justify slavery and those used to justify abortion.

> Sadly, Americans indulged in the lie that the black man was not a person and could therefore be treated as a thing. It is remarkable that exactly the same argument was used in the Roe v Wade decision of 1973 to legalize abortion. One hundred and fifty years ago the black man could be enslaved because he was not legally a person; in the last ten years twelve million unborn children have been killed because the Supreme Court decided they were not persons.[3]

Notwithstanding the extreme seriousness of this issue, which in the UK has led to 1 in 5 pregnancies now ending in abortion, it is only one example in the life of one nation of what the devil can do.

With hindsight it is far more possible to see with the natural eye how the devil has acted. Yet it takes spiritual perception to see it in the moment. So it is in the lives of

individuals. Even for Christians, it requires a special gift
of spiritual sight to discern where they may be, at least to
some extent, the prisoners of their nation, or their social
class, or their group interest. The nature of the devil's
beguiling power is to operate even more under the veil of
distraction than overtly through vile destruction. Human
eyes can see the latter. The former requires the type of
eyesight Jesus alone can give, especially as His influence
operates around our personal lives.

In *The Screwtape Letters*, C.S. Lewis gave this well-
known warning.

> There are two equal and opposite errors into which
> our race can fall about the devils. One is to disbelieve
> in their existence. The other is to believe, and to feel
> an excessive and unhealthy interest in them. They
> themselves are equally pleased by both errors and
> hail a materialist or a magician with the same
> delight.[4]

Whereas Lewis implied the danger fifty years ago was in
getting caught in either one error or the other, nowadays
the risk is as much in the both/and as in the either/or.

In the area of evil spirits possessing individuals, the
interest of at least a proportion of the Christian community has become unhealthy and excessive. The devil
has had to concede ground on the exposure this has
brought. His *quid pro quo* however has been to lure
others into disbelief about the possibility of his influence
upon their lives. We all need to be able to see through
the spiritual smoke screen to understand where we are
being beguiled. First for our own healing, but secondly
that we may be able to minister healing to others as
they seek deliverance, not necessarily from literal evil
spirits, but from the attitudes which reflect the particular
beguiling influence on each of us that comes from behind
the spiritual smoke screen.

One simple question demonstrates the need for us to

cry out to Jesus for revelation of this, as Bartimaeus had the courage to cry out through the crowd. Why are we all, with few exceptions, not more radical in our Christian commitment? The answers that can be given point in the same direction. Either we are blind to our responsibility to share the gospel with non-Christians, or we are blind about their eternal destiny. Or we are blind to the fact that we can't be bothered. Or we are more concerned with other things. Somehow we have been beguiled into thinking that it's not all that important to share our faith with others.

The fact is that we are blind. Our eyes may have been opened to the reality of Jesus as Saviour and that in His name demons flee. It is a delusion however to think that this means that no more spiritual blindness remains. There is a far bigger deliverance ministry which is needed than that to do with expelling demons. It is to do with deliverance from spiritual blindness. Demonomania has served as a very powerful distraction from this reality. If we are to mature in the ministry of healing, we need to greatly tighten up our understanding of the presence of 'spirits' and how they are to be dealt with.

When Bartimaeus was delivered from his blindness, we are told he then followed Jesus along the road. The purpose of having our spiritual eyesight increasingly restored is that we too might be better able to follow behind Jesus on the road He would lead us along. That road takes us through the smoke screen, into the place where the holds of the devil may be truly exposed for what they are, that healing in its very fullest sense may be both ministered and received.

When Is A Problem Psychological?

More and more I begin to realize that a mature ministry of healing depends on the ability to handle the tough question of how to distinguish between three categories of need. Firstly, what is demonic, in the sense of the presence of a spirit which needs to be expelled. Secondly, what is psychological or behavioural for which personal responsibility has to be taken in order that the way might be made open for healing to come; and thirdly, what is psychosomatic, which requires ministry to a person's total being. We turn now to consider the psychological category.

It is Jesus alone who can enable us to have spiritual perception of the devil's strategies, particularly in the psychological area. He can do this because of the victory he won in the desert following His baptism. It was not only a spiritual victory over the devil, but also a psychological one. If the devil was going to use his best methods anywhere, it was there. However, Jesus exposed them for what they were. He unmasked the subtlety of the devil's psychological tactics, designed to lure us into behaviour we don't even appreciate the significance of, but through which he can get us into bondage.

The temptation followed Jesus' fast of forty days and nights. After this:

The tempter came to him and said, 'If you are the Son of God, tell these stones to become bread.'
Jesus answered, 'It is written: "Man does not live

on bread alone, but on every word that comes from
the mouth of God."'

Then the devil took him to the holy city and had
him stand on the highest point of the temple. 'If you
are the Son of God,' he said, 'throw yourself down.
For it is written:

"He will command his angels concerning you,
    and they will lift you up in their hands,
so that you will not strike your foot against a
    stone."'

Jesus answered him, 'It is also written: "Do not
put the Lord your God to the test."'

Again, the devil took him to a very high mountain
and showed him all the kingdoms of the world and
their splendour. 'All this I will give you,' he said, 'if
you will bow down and worship me.'

Jesus said to him, 'Away from me, Satan! For it
is written: "Worship the Lord your God, and serve
him only."'

(Matthew 4:3–11)

The way the three temptations were put to Jesus obviously related to the uniqueness of His position. Yet
through them Jesus exposed the chief areas the devil
most favours for gaining a hold over human beings, and
the means by which he seeks to do it. Jesus' mission
was to bring healing and wholeness to the world. The
devil's goal was to defeat the Son of God in the crucial
areas where He would save mankind from what most
ensnares him. Because the devil is uncreative, we may
be assured he has come up with nothing new in the last
two thousand years. Where Jesus most wants us healed,
is where the devil most seeks his hold.

Though the devil decisively lost that contest in the
wilderness, he presses on with seeking exactly the same
holds on people today as then. It is an impoverishment
to the present-day healing ministry that it does not
draw as much insight from the victory Jesus won in

the wilderness as it does from the accounts of how Jesus ministered healing. Yet they are surely an equal, if not even more illuminating, picture of how Jesus came to destroy the works of the devil. In the wilderness, Jesus exposed what the bottom line of the battle was as far as the devil was concerned. What it provides is a 'from the bottom up' understanding of what the fullness of healing is about, rather than a 'from the top down' understanding which may be drawn from studying the stories of how Jesus ministered healing.

The clues to the depth of the healing Jesus came to bring, and which the devil wanted to prove He would be unable to bring, are to be found in what underlies the three temptations rather than in what is to be seen on the surface. We need to remember that before anything else, the devil is crafty and subtle (Genesis 3:1). At first sight the three temptations look anything other than subtle. Superficially, they are gauche, but this is the devil's style. Demonic possession for example is gauche, and if this distracts us from recognizing that his primary style is the subtle catch, this suits him well. His strategy is invariably to seek to grasp our superficial attraction in order to mask the hold he is really after.

His goal is to get the type of hold on people that goes unnoticed, such that they have no perception of the depth of need for deliverance from it. Yet for such a hold to constrain them far beyond that which they appreciated, from living out the radical nature of the gospel. The replies Jesus gave to each temptation exposed the nature of those holds, and the subtlety with which the devil seeks to apply them. They also point to the depth of the healing which Jesus came to bring. This may be summarized under three headings which were the focal points of the temptations – the satisfaction of our appetites, the need to be in control of our situation, and the direction of our worship.

Deliverance from appetite satisfaction

Just as the first Adam succumbed through an appeal to his appetite, so the devil made his first attempt on Jesus, as the last Adam. This was where he had first won and where he had been winning ever since. This then was where he wanted his first victory against Jesus. The temptation after forty days of fasting may have been presented mockingly – 'You, the Son of God, hungry!', but most likely it was presented seductively – 'It's what you deserve after all this time.' A line familiar to us all as we face the pressure to satisfy the demands of our appetites designed in such a way so as to distract us from the spiritual cost of doing so.

We need to keep in mind that it was, however, the Holy Spirit who had led Jesus into this temptation. This was in fact battle on God's terms, not the devil's. God's purpose was that, as the representative and saviour of His people, Jesus would reclaim that which was lost in Eden. It was there that the gift of appetite had become inverted. The effect of sin was to turn the primary focus of it from God to self. All sin is ultimately rooted in appetite distortion, which in one way or another seeks satisfaction for self. For healing to be able to comprehensively deal with the damage sin has wreaked, Jesus had to defeat the control of a person's life which the appetite had usurped. Not just to reclaim it, but to refocus it first and foremost on God.

Jesus' reply penetrated through to what the bottom line of the temptation really was. It was not about something as tawdry as whether or not He would use a miracle to appease His hunger. His reference to Moses' words in Deuteronomy 8:3, that 'man does not live on bread alone, but on every word that comes from the mouth of the Lord', exposed what it was really probing. The context of those words was God's dealings with the people of Israel. In the previous verse, Moses had urged them to 'remember how the Lord your God led you all the way in the desert these forty years, to humble you and to test you in order to know

what was in your heart, whether or not you would keep
his commands.'

Jesus was pinpointing the connection between the
heart and the body. It is not when our appetites are
satisfied that we discover what truly rules our hearts.
It is only when there is lack of satisfaction that the truth
emerges about what really matters most. Though there is
a right and proper fulfilment of every appetite we have,
each one has its flip side, which can exercise enormous
power should it not be satisfied. The central issue for
every human being is whether hunger for God is greater
than the sum total of our other hungers.

Richard Foster in *Money, Sex and Power* speaks of the
demonic potential in the appetite in each of these three
areas.

> The demon in money is greed. Nothing can destroy
> human beings like the passion to possess. The demon
> in sex is lust. True sexuality leads to humanness,
> but lust leads to depersonalization. Lust capti-
> vates rather than emancipates, devours rather than
> nourishes. The demon in power is pride. True power
> has as its aim to set people free, whereas pride
> is determined to dominate. True power enhances
> relationships; pride destroys them.[1]

Though he emphasizes that his reference to demons, and
the need for their exorcism, is purely metaphorical, the
language he uses is highly appropriate. Appetites in the
right place can be of great blessing, but in the hands
of the evil realm become a curse from which we need
deliverance.

Jesus laid bare the devil's aim to have our appetite
fulfilment under his influence in the most subtle way. His
style is to make it all seem so legitimate, but to actually
hamstring us by the fulfilment of them. His target is that
the energy, initiative and every other resource we have,

which could be released into a radical relationship with God, gets diverted into the fulfilment of our needs. His target is that we might think we are living as disciples whilst actually putting our comfort zone first. Yet it is through subtle distraction from the extent of our need for appetite fulfilment that he seeks to get us into such delusion.

In the context of the society we live in, we may genuinely be living more simply than our neighbours. However, the devil still has us under his deception if we only use the standards of the society we live in as the benchmark of how free we are. Those standards reflect the insidious combination of commercialism, materialism and the desire for instant gratification which characterizes our Western society. It accommodates a permissiveness which scorns moral restraint and demands its rights whilst sitting light on its responsibilities. It is a society caught up in the devil's Catch-22 of getting the minimum of satisfaction out of the maximum of attention, which drives the consumer ever onwards. Like the effect of sea water on those who drink it, the way Western society satisfies its appetites only increases the thirst for more.

Living amidst it, the scope to be sucked in is enormous. We may say, for example, 'It's not that I'm greedy, it's just that I'd like a better standard of living for my family.' Surrounding influences can so readily distract us from the spiritual price involved in what looks like legitimate appetite satisfaction. It is so easy to lose sight of the lesson to be drawn from the history of the church, with its vastly better track record in the face of persecution than when its appetites have been fulfilled. To receive spiritual eyes, which can see through the subtle bondage that lies in appetite fulfilment, does not make persecution of itself any less unpleasant. However, the witness of the church through the ages has been that it is a price worth paying.

To understand healing 'from the bottom up', where the battle began in the wilderness, is the starting point for such understanding. It begins in the healing of the orientation of our appetites, to turn them not superficially, but in totality, from sin and self to God. Persecution is not obligatory for us to get the revelation of how much we really need this healing. However, the power of appetite fulfilment to distract, and eventually to delude, is such that it may take at least 'bad' circumstances and perhaps even persecution, to bring home the things which matter and the things which don't. It is for many only then that they truly realize the sort of sight they need to cry out to Jesus for.

Healing 'from the bottom up', is therefore about the fundamental re-direction of hearts such that they will not compromise their relationship with God for the sake of the flesh. This is not asceticism, simply about the greatest hunger of all being for God. As David said 'My soul thirsts for you, my body longs for you, in a dry and weary land where there is no water' (Psalm 63:1). The fullness of healing is reflected by the place of hunger for God, regardless of whether the other appetites are first fulfilled. In this lies the healing of all that happened in Eden. It was this the devil tried to stop Jesus from bringing. It is this that the devil still seeks to stop us from receiving.

Deliverance from the need to be in control

In the second temptation, Jesus was tempted to throw Himself off the highest point of the temple. It was, however, about far more than the possibility of securing a large following through a spectacular proof that He really was the Messiah.

The scripture His reply was based on, again cut through to what the devil was really going for. The context of the words 'It is also written: 'Do not put the Lord your God to the test' (Deuteronomy 6:16) was that of the people of Israel putting God to the test at Massah. They had camped where there was no water to drink, and had

begun to quarrel with Moses, to the extent that he
thought they were ready to stone him. God told him
to strike the rock at Horeb with the staff with which
he struck the Nile, that water would come out for the
people. Moses called the place Massah (meaning testing)
and Meribah (meaning quarrelling) because the Israelites
tested the Lord saying 'Is the Lord among us, or not?'
(Exodus 17:7).

Jesus perceived that the devil was seeking to draw Him
into confrontation with the Father. He was being tempted
to both test the Father and quarrel with Him. First about
the way in which He was to convince the world of His
Messiahship, and second about where control lay in the
way He was to bring salvation to the world. The devil's
aim was to prevent Jesus from being able to heal the
inversion of our appetites from hunger for God to self-
satisfaction and sin. Ultimately it was to lure Him into
replaying what happened in Eden, which was rebellion.
Man was created to live His life under God's control, but
in Eden he declared that he knew best and that he would
control his own life from there on.

Today we live in a society where control of one's circumstances has a high premium placed upon it. It is the very
reasonableness of it that distracts from what it can lead
to. Demonic strategy is to get man into the place where
he replays what went on in Eden, to declare afresh that
his destiny is in his own hands rather than God's. How
it happens may not seem like rebellion, yet the exercise
of control can be a slippery slope into spiritual rebellion
which isn't even noticed.

Control of our private lives to keep out that which
might disturb us can seem so reasonable at face value.
The existence of technology that controls the systems
which provide the infrastructure of our lives can seem
so beneficial. The advances of science and medicine that
will enable the circumstances of life to be increasingly
controlled, in order to apparently improve the standard
of our lives, looks to be so worth having. Yet it is

through the attractiveness of control that we can be
so easily distracted from its catch. In the capacity to
exercise control lies the danger that man increasingly
sees himself as his own god and his own saviour. Far
from having won freedom, when mankind sees himself
this way, as he does far more than he ever realizes, he
has put himself under a fearsome form of bondage from
which he is utterly unable to save himself.

Central to the healing Jesus came to bring was the
setting free of mankind from the consequences of that
first declaration in Eden – and every subsequent one –
that he would do it 'his way'. The only way the devil
could stop Him was to tempt Him to do what would
wrest control from the Father. If He would do that which
would force the Father to act, however much attention
He might have drawn to Himself, He would have made
Himself as one of us. No longer would He be able to save
us. Jesus saw through it and resisted. Because He did
so, we may be set free from the need to be in control,
and right relationship with God such as existed before
the Fall, may be re-established.

How much that healing is needed in our lives is
something we only see by revelation. True conversion
is the surrender of control to Almighty God. Though
we may say that this is what we have done, the reality
does not instantly match the reputation. The Christian
life is about becoming 'powerfully powerless'. It is about
'Abandonment to the Divine Providence' as Jean-Pierre
de Caussade entitled it. At the time of commitment to
Christ we make a beginning in that direction. Yet the
tendency is to still want the evidence that God is doing
what we think He should be. We may no longer be in overt
rebellion with God, but the likelihood is that we are still
naming our terms.

It may take some duress to expose it, but like the
people of Israel, when things go wrong, the tendency
is to start asking 'Is the Lord among us, or not?' This
simply demonstrates the depth of healing that is needed

from the consequences of the spiritual rebellion in our lives. The potential remains within all of us to test God and quarrel with Him. The healing of our need to be in control, to have things our way, is central to the healing of our entire being. It is also the key to our potential for being used of God being more fully released. Perhaps this is why the devil continues to use the spectacular to tempt us away from seeing how much we need to receive such healing.

Deliverance from idolatry

Having defeated him twice, Jesus was then able to flush out the supreme temptation that the devil would use. The fact that the devil left Jesus after the third temptation proved he had played his biggest card. It was in the offering the kingdoms of the world to Jesus in return for His bowing down and worshipping him, that the devil exposed his most subtle strategy of all. As with the previous two, there was far more below the surface of the temptation than appeared.

At His baptism which directly preceded the temptations, the voice from heaven had said 'This is my Son, whom I love; with him I am well pleased' (Matthew 3:17). It was a fulfilment of the words of the psalmist who centuries earlier had written 'I will proclaim the decree of the Lord: He said to me, 'You are my Son; today I have become your Father. Ask of me, and I will make the nations your inheritance, the ends of the earth your possession' (Psalm 2:7–8). Jesus already had the promise from God of what the devil was offering. Superficially, the temptation offered was the crown without the way of the cross. However, Jesus' response again cut through to the yet-greater seriousness of what the devil was actually seeking to do.

He replied 'Away from me, Satan! For it is written: 'Worship the Lord your God, and serve him only.' It was a reference to Moses' words to the people of Israel which

warned them not to follow other gods, for 'the Lord your
God, who is among you, is a jealous God and his anger will
burn against you, and he will destroy you from the face
of the land' (Deuteronomy 6:15). The devil's strategy has
always been the lure of idolatry, even for God's people. If
he succeeds, he gets them under the wrath of God, which
can result in their spiritual destruction. In this case it was
for the Son of God as well. It was not just the avoidance of
the cross he was trying to lure Jesus into, it was the total
destruction of who He was that the devil was seeking.

His aim is no less extreme for every one of us, and his
strategy no different. It is to distract us from seeing the
subtle hold idolatry can have on our lives, and the degree
of spiritual destruction that lies within it. The more we
buy into it, the more it has power to blind us to the basic
fact about mankind. This is that we have been created
as worshipping beings who, as a car runs on petrol, run
on worship. The question the devil most seeks to keep
us from considering is who or what we worship? In the
answer to that question lies the balance of spiritual life
or death.

As worshipping creatures, mankind needs a centre
outside himself. Through this he finds meaning, worth
and significance. Fallenness has caused mankind to want
gods of his own making, which he can create and control.
Those gods may not be wrong things in themselves, but
can simply be good things in the wrong place. One
definition of an idol is 'that which rivets my attention,
centres my activity, preoccupies my mind and motivates
my action'.[2] Thus even potentially wholesome things
like family, health, beauty, sex, possessions, career, and
money, can become idols.

In the parable of the banquet (Matthew 22:1–14) the
master's anger was not that those who were invited had
possessions, but that their possessions had so entangled
them they were unable to come. Such is the effect of
an idol, that it possesses its owner in a way which goes
unnoticed, but binds them. Just as no one notices that

they have become attached to a chair until they try to get up out of it, so it is with idols. The attachment goes unnoticed until the attempt is made to get free of them.

The devil's strategy continues to be to work very hard at distracting us from recognizing the extent to which idols still have hold in our lives, and the power they have to destroy us spiritually. Some missionary friends working in Japan described how their landlord had made a commitment to Christ, but hadn't as yet seen the need to get rid of the family Shinto god-shelf. The inconsequentiality of the Western church suggests that we may be more like that man than we realize. Conversion is about turning 'to God from idols to serve the living and true God' (1 Thessalonians 1:9). The presentation of the gospel as a few simple things to believe, and a decision to be made, leaves many blind to the unrenounced idolatry that remains amongst us.

John and Paula Sandford, in *Healing the Wounded Spirit*, have described the presence of idolatry this way.

> There is no sin which does not involve idolatry. If we steal, we have valued whatever we took more than we valued God. If we commit adultery, we have elevated that woman or that man as more important to us than God. If we choose not to be in church on Sunday, we have made an idol of whatever we wanted more than obedience – pleasure, business, repairing the house, laziness, etc. If we do not tithe, mammon is our god, no matter what we say.[3]

Idolatry comes in many guises, including covetousness and greed (Colossians 3:5). However, the Sandfords argue that behind every other idolatry is one worse than all, which lies at the core of all of us. 'It is the kingdom of self, where self rules all our hidden motives. The throne may be given to Jesus, but self still fancies itself the power behind His throne.'[4] They go on to speak of what is at the core of us being so evil it cannot be resolved, only slain. It is determined to be like God. This is why idolatry incurs such wrath from God, and why the devil works so hard to smoke screen its effect upon us.

The crescendo of the devil's temptation of Jesus was the attempt to get Him to succumb to idolatry. It was not just to stop Him going the way of the cross that we might be saved from destruction. It was that He Himself might be destroyed. Jesus saw through the extent to which the devil will use idolatry to secure the greatest spiritual destruction possible. He resisted it and won not only the spiritual but also the psychological victory. The devil departed.

A mature ministry of healing needs to be able to minister the benefits of both aspects of that victory. First it needs to be able to work out where we have to take personal responsibility for the behavioural choices we have made, without shifting the blame onto anything else demonic or psychosomatic. It must expose the bondage to sin which wrongful appetite satisfaction leads to, the spiritual rebellion that the need to be in control is actually about and, most of all, the spiritual destructiveness that follows on from idolatry. Only then can spiritual victory be ministered.

11

When Is Healing Psychosomatic?

One of the curious but inescapable facts about the ministry of healing is the way in which those being ministered to appear to expose the minimum number of symptoms necessary to secure healing. I was no exception. The defence systems of my subconscious seemed to work with cunning to ensure that no more than was necessary was given away about what I'm actually like deep down. Something in me suspected that the treatment which could be prescribed for sorting me out might be too radical for comfort!

Spiritually or medically, to expect the fullness of healing to result from the presentation of only a limited number of symptoms is naive. All it can result in is the equivalent of skimming off the part of an iceberg that juts out above the surface of the sea. It is a vain task. However successful the skimming off might be, the nature of an iceberg is such that the next part of the nine-tenths which lies below the surface will then bob to the surface. Slice that bit off and another bit will appear, and so on. Icebergs are only handled by coming to terms with the full extent of what lies beneath the surface. So it is with us as people.

This poses the question of whether healing can ever be more than superficial unless the full diagnosis of what lies beneath the surface is faced. To receive any real depth of healing, do we therefore first need to be set free to be free not just in our body, but in the whole of the psychosomatic beings that we are? A lesson from history suggests we do.

When on New Year's Day, 1863, President Abraham
Lincoln signed 'The Emancipation Proclamation', he was
announcing that four million Negro slaves were to be
freed. No longer would they be under the evil scourge of
bondage to their masters as chattels who had no choice
but to do their bidding, however humiliating it was. By
December, 1865, the Constitution of the United States of
America was amended, and slavery was finally abolished.
It was a victory won at great cost, involving the death of
650,000 young men in the Civil War, and subsequently
the assassination of Lincoln himself. Yet the staggering
fact is that the vast majority of all the slaves who were
legally freed stayed under the tyrannical dominion of
their masters. They continued slaving on the plantations
of the South to the end of their days. Something more was
needed than a declaration in principle. They themselves
needed to make a decision in practice to go. It meant
leaving behind all that was familiar. It meant choosing
to die to their old identity. It meant stepping out to go a
new way.

From our perspective, we may be incredulous that they
should choose to remain under the vile regime of slavery.
One explanation is that they were a people whose will had
been crushed through being so cruelly subjected as slaves.
They had no grasp of what freedom was, let alone where
to go. Yet there was more to it than that. At work within
the hearts of those legally-freed slaves was the same that
is within us all. It is a fundamental unwillingness, even
a fear, of allowing death to the old identity be worked
out, not just in principle, but in practice, whatever the
apparent benefits.

For many Christians, the effect of this is that we remain
in bondage to our unhealed identities, without the reality
of the freedom the gospel promises. Just as it was not only
those emancipated slaves who lost out on their healing,
but also the whole nation of America which suffered the
ongoing presence of slavery long after it was legally
abolished, so there is a parallel for us. Not only do we

lose out on the fullness of the opportunity afforded to us personally, but the world around us is deprived of the healing influence that could be exercised through us.

It requires a determined decision to die to what underlies our old patterns of behaviour. There is much within us that wants to cling to the old ways. We desire freedom in principle. We want the inconvenient symptoms of an unhealed self to be dealt with. Yet only insofar as the inner self doesn't have to die too much in practice. We want the benefits of change, just as long as not a lot within is altered. It is only when we recognize how much this mentality which controls us needs dealing with, that we can begin to enter into the spiritual freedom that Jesus paid such a price for us to have. If we do not, the tragedy is that it is not just we who lose out. It is also those who through us God wants to minister healing to, healing which touches not just symptoms, but goes to the very roots of their being.

Healing of body, soul and spirit

To see why we can be so reluctant to receive the fullness of the spiritual health God has for us, we need to consider how healing operates in us as 'trichotomous' beings; that is beings who have a body, a soul and a spirit. 1 Thessalonians 5:23 speaks of God's power to 'sanctify you through and through. May your whole spirit, soul and body be kept blameless at the coming of our Lord Jesus Christ.' Theologians have long debated how to define the soul and the spirit, given their interchangeability in Scripture and the psychosomatic unity of our natures. However, a clear separation of them demonstrates how the fullness of healing comes to the different aspects of our being in quite distinctive ways.

If we limit the definition of our spirit to that unique identity each of us has before God, and our soul to the complex of functions which comprises our personality, such as our will, emotions, mental faculties, conscience

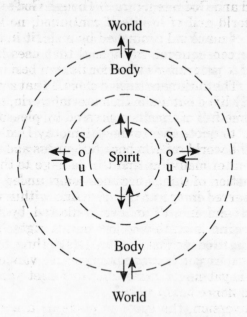

Fig. 1   Mankind before the Fall

etc., then, albeit simplistically, we can picture our nature in the form of three concentric circles (see figure 1). Mankind was created primarily to operate out of his spirit, which was to be in an harmonious, worshipful relationship with God. The soul was to be shaped by the desires of the spirit, in effect to be its vehicle for expressing that relationship with God. It was endued with creative ability, so that mankind might live as a creator made in the image of its Creator. Creative living was to be expressed through the physical body as it interacted with a world created and sustained by God.

The consequence of the Fall was separation from God leading to spiritual death. This did not mean that mankind ceased to exist spiritually, just as a telephone line does not cease to exist when we say its gone dead. There was however a break in the spiritual connection between mankind and God (see figure 2) Though God's sustenance of the world and of life itself continued, no longer was the soul of mankind controlled by a spirit in touch with God. The consequence was a soul that uses its creative potential to programme itself for its own best interests as it sees it. The sinful and selfish choices that are made are physically lived out amidst a material world, such that it has become full of 'spirits oppressed by pleasure, wealth and care' to quote the words of Timothy Dudley-Smith's hymn. The world reflects back fallenness and selfishness to the soul of mankind, and the damage to the soul and its perception of things becomes compounded.

The marred image of God remains within the soul of mankind and is still in part reflected by the world, but mankind is unable to get things right by his own efforts. So, to quote Pascal, 'Man is a dethroned monarch, cast down from his former eminence, vanquished and depraved, yet never quite able to forget what he once was, and hence ought to be.'

At conversion, the spirit is made as a new creation. 'The old has gone, the new has come,' (2 Corinthians 5:17). That, however, only applies to the spirit. The soul still has plenty of the old within which is determined to beat anything else which it sees vying for influence. A profound conflict results. There is the old pattern of self-interest, fuelled by the influence of a selfish world, operating on the wounded perceptions and recollections of life experience. On the other hand there is the influence of the new creation spirit, in tune with the holiness of Almighty God. What is to prevail?

This conflict is so excellently described by Paul when he writes in Romans 7:15 'I do not understand what I do. For what I want to do I do not do, but what I hate I do.' It is not now just a vague sense within that we ought to be better, but an acute awareness of it being our personal choice as to whether we are better or not. We now have the option to go the way of Jesus, not just in principle, but in practice. What determines it is how

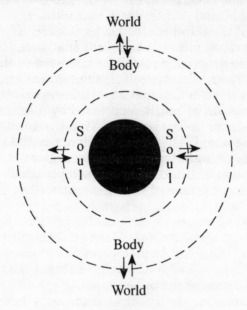

Fig. 2   Mankind after the Fall

open we are to the process of healing in our souls which
only the prescription of dying to self can yield.

Though the sanctification of body, soul and spirit will
all be complete at the coming of our Lord Jesus Christ,
it is crucial to see that they will reach completion by
three different routes. Our spirits have already died as
the result of sin. The only choice which remains for us is
whether or not we will receive the free gift of new life for
them through which alone they can be healed. If we have,
the healing of our spirit is already complete. By total
contrast, our bodies will only be completely healed after
we physically die. Then what was sown as a natural body
will be raised as a spiritual body (1 Corinthians 15:44).
Only then will there be no more weeping and no more
pain (Revelation 21:4). That death and healing has yet to
come. For the present, even the most spectacular healing

of our bodies is no more than a provisional token of what is to come, the timing of which we have little choice in. The healing of our souls however is a different matter altogether.

Heels and soles, or healed souls?

The process for the healing of our soul lies between that of the spirit and that of the body. Something somewhere within it must have already died to itself for conversion to have taken place, and even in the newest believer at least some measure of healing within it will have happened as a result. Although the complete healing of our soul will not take place until after our physical death, it is nonetheless up to us as to how much more healing of it through dying to itself will take place whilst we are still in this world.

The premise that so easily creeps into the healing ministry is that it is essentially all about the repair of what was once good. In physical healing, that can on occasion be all that it is about. However in the healing of the soul – inner healing as it is often called – that can be a very dangerous assumption. If the supposition is made that our souls can be patched like a pair of shoes at the cobblers, then the process of exposing and putting to death what needs to be slain in it can be totally missed. The gospel is not about patching up the old, nor about pouring new wine into old wineskins (Matthew 9:16,17). It is about nothing less than death and resurrection.

Jesus did not come to improve us by patching us up. He came that we might know His resurrection life. There is only one way this happens, which is by our uniting with Him in His death, that we can be united with Him in His resurrection (Romans 6:5). Paul testifies to what this means in practice in Galatians 2:20 'I have been crucified with Christ and I no longer live, but Christ lives in me. The life I live in the body, I live by faith in the Son of God, who loved me and gave himself for me.' It is because the heart is so devious that what it naturally seeks is nothing more than the patching up of the holes. It's ploy is in the most subtle way to enable those long-running strongholds to remain unexposed, that the depth of their evil influence in our lives may not be revealed. The need is therefore not to patch up the holes, but the opposite, to dig in and expose what lies behind them. Far more than we may realize can be there, as God once revealed to Ezekiel in a vision.

The revelation God gave to him was about idolatry in the Temple (Ezekiel 8:1–13). In the vision, Ezekiel was brought to the entrance of the court of the Temple. He looked, and saw a hole in the wall. God said to him 'Son of man, now dig into the wall.' So he dug into the wall, and saw a doorway there. God told him to go in and see 'the wicked and detestable things' being done there. As he went in and looked, he saw in the darkness the extent of the idolatry being secretly practised by the elders of the house of Israel. It would have been much easier to have patched the hole in the wall. However, it was only as the hole was opened up and courage exercised to go in, that what needed to be put to death was exposed for what it was.

We are the temple of the Holy Spirit, and for the fullness of health in our souls, we need similar revelation of the doorways to the dark places in them where the detestable things exist. Alexander Solzhenitsyn put it this way. 'Good and evil are never distinguished by lines on a map. The line separating good and evil passes not through states, nor between classes, nor between political parties, but right through every human heart.' It is not pleasant to have what lies on the other side of the line of evil that runs through our hearts exposed for what it is. All too easily we can go with the subtle strategy of the old self. By acknowledging that there are some holes, we hope that in patching them up the doorways to what actually lies behind, that needs putting to death, may be covered up.

The battle therefore rages between our new creation

spirit which seeks the submission of the soul to what it witnesses to, and the demand of the soul to be able to continue to be allowed to 'do it my way'. At the coming of the Lord, we will be sanctified through and through in body, soul and spirit. Before then, we have been given, through the grace of Jesus, the potential to become in our souls what we already are in our spirits. It depends on a personal choice to mortify that which is not holy within us.

Unfortunately, the 'Just as I am' type of conversion which a significant proportion of our evangelism results in, may not have established understanding of how salvation comes to our souls, as distinct from our spirits. The convert may have been set free from sin in principle, but not in practice. Like many owners said to their slaves following the Emancipation Proclamation 'I don't care what changes there have been in the law, you're still under my control,' so the devil speaks to God's people, and he gets listened to.

Scripture is uncompromising about what needs to be done for the healing of the soul, and who must do it.

> Put to death, therefore, whatever belongs to your earthly nature: sexual immorality, impurity, lust, evil desires and greed, which is idolatry . . . you must rid yourselves of all such things as these: anger, rage, malice, slander and filthy language from your lips.
> (Colossians 3:5–8)

The temptation is, however to compromise by putting on 'compassion, kindness, humility, gentleness and patience, forgiveness and over all these . . . love' (v12–14) without the ruthless eradication of what we had on before. Whether it is the new that is gone for, through dying to the old, or whether it is just a patched-up version of the old, depends on how much freedom there is to be free. So the healing of the soul is affected by the type of healing the spirit has received. Being the psychosomatic unity that we are, freedom to receive healing in the body can in turn depend on the healing the soul has known.

It was for this reason that the early Church ensured that every new convert was not only free from sin in principle, but knew what it was to be able to walk away from sin in practice. Doubtless this enabled the ministry of healing to also be exercised with much greater effectiveness.

The scrutiny of the early church

In the initial years of the church, baptism was a part of the announcement of the good news. To submit to the gospel was to submit to baptism, and to submit to baptism was to submit to the gospel. There was no delay in its administration, no course of preparation, and no sifting of candidates. However, the context of those days needs to be appreciated. It was simply not possible to associate with the church without being willing to put everything at stake. It was clear that to identify with Jesus Christ meant that some form of persecution was quite probable, and martyrdom possible. Notwithstanding the personal issues which may still have needed working through, to become one of the people of the Way presupposed a willingness to die to self, not just in principle, but in practice.

By the third century things had changed substantially. Conversion was the starting point, but it was more like the key to the door, rather than the door to the house. Each candidate for baptism went through a three-year period of probation, known as the catechumenate. Those who wished to be accepted for it were stringently examined for their motives, their condition in life and their morals. During this period of time they were regularly instructed, and it was used as a period of moral testing. At the end of it they were assessed to see if there was sufficient evidence of faith and moral uprightness to warrant proceeding. Only those who were approved were allowed to enrol for the six weeks of intensive preparation for baptism at Easter.

During those forty days, the candidates received three hours instruction every day, they were obliged to fast, and to keep night vigils. Exorcisms were pronounced over them daily, that the devil's power might be gradually weakened and broken. They also had to go through the scrutinies, which were public occasions, when the candidate underwent exorcisms of exceptional severity, in circumstances of some humiliation, standing naked and barefoot upon goatskins. The aim was to see if the candidate could endure the scrutiny without showing any signs of continuing demon-possession. Candidates were left in no doubt as to what it meant to declare the words 'I renounce Satan and all his angels, and all his service, all his vain pomps and all his worldly allurements. I commit myself to Jesus Christ and pledge allegiance to Him. I believe, and ask to be baptized in the name of the Father, and of the Son, and of the Holy Spirit.'

The impact of such preparation on Cyprian, a rich and cultured man of Carthage, the chief city of Roman Africa, is related by Anne Field OSB.[1] She tells how in AD 246 he wrote to his friend Donatus:

> I was completely involved in this world's affairs, influenced by all its changing moods and troubles, and exiled from the light of truth. I had indeed been told that God offered men and women a second birth by which we could be saved, but I very much doubted I could change the kind of life I was then living. Frankly, I could not see how a person could cast off his fallen nature and be changed in heart and soul, while he still lived in the same body as before. How is it possible, I asked myself, to change the habits of a lifetime instantaneously? How can one suddenly rid oneself of accumulated guilt and break with sin that has become so deeply rooted in one's life? Can a man whose whole life style is

characterized by feasting and luxury learn frugality and simplicity in a single moment? A person who craves for public distinction and honours cannot bear to be passed over unnoticed; another who is accustomed to throngs of flattering attendants thinks it a terrible penance to be left alone. Is every species of temptation suddenly to lose its force? Shall we no longer feel the enticement of wine and good living? Will pride no longer swell our heads or anger blaze in our breasts? Shall we no longer be troubled by covetousness or cruelty or ambition or lust? These were my thoughts. My past life was burdened with so many sins that I saw no way ever to be rid of, that I had grown accustomed to giving in to my weakness. I despaired of ever being any better. Consequently I simply humoured my evil inclinations and made no attempt to combat them. But at last I made up my mind to ask for baptism. I went down into those life-giving waters, and all the stains of my past life were washed away. I committed my life to the Lord; He cleansed my heart and filled me with His Holy Spirit. I was born again, a new man.

Cyprian's testimony of his addictive behaviour before his baptism shows how there is little that is new in the behaviour of mankind. It also shows the potential there is to be totally set free of it when the axe is put to the root of it in the name of Jesus. In consequence of his baptism, Cyprian so dedicated himself to celibacy, poverty and the Bible that within two years he was made Bishop of Carthage. Ten years later he was martyred for his faith. Whatever we might make of daily exorcisms and public scrutinies, the story of Cyprian demonstrates the degree of potential there is for the healing of the souls of those who are truly open to it.

A mature model of healing needs to take account of the extent to which we are a psychosomatic unity. However, it will never be able to compensate for the lack of wellbeing which is rooted in inadequate spiritual initiation into the Christian faith. Even Sartre, the nihilist, commented that 'no man is truly alive until he has something to die for'. For the Christian, there is a vitality in the body which alone comes from having truly died and been raised to newness of life in the spirit.

'When Christ calls a man,' wrote Dietrich Bonhoeffer, 'he bids him come and die.' In *The Cost of Discipleship* he explains the continuing nature of the process of death to self like this.

> Self-denial is never just a series of isolated acts of mortification or asceticism. It is not suicide, for there is an element of self-will even in that. To deny oneself is to be aware only of Christ and no more of self, to see only Him who goes before and no more the road which is too hard for us. Once more, all that self-denial can say is: 'He leads the way, keep close to Him'.[2]

When there is health in the soul, then not only is there basis for ministering healing to the body, but the relative importance of physical health lessens. Until the church rediscovers something of its earlier practices of initiation, if its practice of healing is to mature, it may well need to develop the art of 'remedial initiation'. Without this, the ministry of healing will not be able to be appropriately psychosomatic – capable of touching the complex interrelationships that comprise the whole of our being. Let alone have an effective foundation for healing which reaches beyond individuals and out into the complexities of society.

12

Is Our Healing Ministry Too Privatized?

T hree and a half hours is a long while for any service,
let alone when it's in a language you don't speak! Yet
that service at the Central Baptist Church, Leningrad,
left an indelible mark on my mind. Though I didn't
realize it then, I was sitting in on a healing service. Not
for individuals, but for a nation. The nation of Russia.

It was the early seventies, when the eyes of the Soviet
system noted even those who attended permitted services
of worship. One man said that though there was no direct
persecution, life somehow overlooked them. Promotion at
work would bypass them, better accommodation would
never be forthcoming, their children would not get on
at school as they ought, and so on. However indirect, it
was still persecution. It cost to be a regular worshipper
there. Yet far from there only being a few die-hards at
the service, it was packed to overflowing, indeed spilling
out into the street.

Written across the faces of those worshippers was a
looking into the 'over and beyond'. The prospect that
within two decades their country would be rid of communism would then have been unthinkable. For them,
freedom from oppression could only be in the 'not yet',
but this did not stop their belief that one day their nation
would be healed. It warranted a risky expression of faith,
and what that cost those saints over the years cannot be
estimated. The consequence though of their faith in God's
power to deliver them can now be seen. It contributed to
the healing of their nation, or at least the opportunity for

it, which the collapse of communism in the Eastern Bloc has afforded.

Though it was easy, feeling as I did, to centre on my own need for healing, the memory of that service posed another tough question for me. Has our vision for the ministry of healing become far too privatized? For that group of saints in Leningrad I had the privilege to be amongst, the healing of their nation had a higher priority than their own immediate comfort. There was an unforgettable quality about their example which discomforted me about the limited perspective on healing we tend to have now. Yet I doubted if many there had any great experience of ministering healing to another individual. What then, in a mature model of healing, should be the balance of emphasis between that which is individual, and that which is corporate?

Certainly, the healing of nations is not something the healing ministry has so far put much emphasis on. But even this is less than the infinitely greater healing that God will ultimately accomplish. His plan is for the reconciliation to Himself of all things, 'whether things on earth or things in heaven' (Colossians 1:20). It is a plan of healing which from where we stand is utterly beyond our comprehension. Yet unless we engage with it at least in some measure, we cannot have a true perspective for the healing of individuals which can so easily preoccupy us.

Some sort of perspective can be attempted by imagining an Empire State Building of healing. The healing of individuals, where the emphasis has mainly been, is just the ground floor. The pinnacle is the making new of all things. One step through the doorway into the expansiveness of the entrance area leaves no doubt about being somewhere very special. Just to venture through the doorway qualifies as a visit to the building. However, the entrance area is as nothing compared with the immensity of the structure above it. Only when the building is ascended can the enthralling experience of its grandeur be increasingly appreciated. Yet the ground floor is not to be despised, for it has one unique feature the whole building depends on – the way in!

So it is with the healing of individuals. It may only be the ground floor in the sky-scraper of God's purposes for healing, but it is the way in.

Everything has to come and go through this doorway. To have taken just one step through it qualifies you as having entered into the realm of healing. Yet no matter how expansive the entrance area seems in itself, it as nothing compared with what is above it. The appreciation of the enthralling grandeur of healing only comes as we move up from ministering healing to individuals into the higher levels of healing. Ultimately towards the pinnacle of all things being made new. The higher the storey, the higher the story of God's purposes in healing. His invitation is to come up with Him, to see even more of the vista of healing that He will accomplish.

He wants us to look out from the higher vantage point in three directions. Outwards, and away from ourselves, that we might glimpse how far He wants His healing love to reach out. Upwards, to the pinnacle, that we might glimpse the height of His purposes for healing, the making of all things new. Downwards, that we might see from above the perspective of the ground floor of healing, rooted in the lives of individuals as they go about their daily business. Most of all, He wants us to see the connection between these three directions of healing.

Just as without the ground floor there can be no pinnacle, so without the healing of individuals, there can be no healing of nations, let alone of all things being made new. Though it is dramatic to peer down on the healing of individuals from above, it is not the only dramatic view to be had. God wants the downward view put into the far greater perspective of the views outwards and upwards. His purposes for healing are infinitely beyond the privatized needs of the individual, with which we so easily become obsessed. Jesus Christ came to bring not just individual healing and salvation. He came also bringing potential for the fullness of God's saving purposes for a lost world to be ministered, not just to, but far more importantly, through, even the likes of us.

God's desire is therefore that we do far more than just visit the ground floor of healing. If we have been used of the Lord to minister healing to another individual, then we have indeed been in the place of healing. That of itself is good. His desire though is that we do so much more than that. His desire is to take us high up from there, and into no less a vision than the healing of the nations, where in the final analysis the heart of His purpose for healing lies.

Scripture concludes with the graphic picture of the river of life flowing from God's throne. On each side of it, as we have already considered, stands the tree of life. Its leaves are for the healing of the nations (Revelation 22:1–2). So there is a place marked out for the nations in the new Jerusalem. They will walk by the light given out by the Lamb, and their glory and honour will be brought into it (Revelation 21:23–26). All that is individually good about each nation will be received in homage. When Jesus stood up on the last day of the Feast of Tabernacles and spoke of streams of living water flowing from within all those who would believe in Him (John 7:37) He was referring to the outpouring of the Holy Spirit which had yet to be given. That outpouring was not just that individuals might be blessed. It was given that whole nations might have the foretaste of the healing which is to come.

Though we do not yet have the fullness of the river, the gift of the Spirit is still for streams of living water to flow through the merest individual. It is what those streams are comprised of, rather than the channels they flow through, that explains the potential we have for healing the situations, if not the nations, in which we live.

The Spirit and the nations

Most often our understanding of the gift of the Spirit
is based on the story of Pentecost. Yet to found our
understanding of it on Acts chapter 2 alone can lead to
a limited, individualistic, and even privatized interpretation of why the Spirit was given. The book of Acts is
the second part of a two-volume work which introduces
the anointing of the Spirit in the first volume. How Luke
makes that introduction has great implication for our
understanding of the work of the Spirit in general, and
of healing in particular.

It comes in his account of Jesus' first rejection in the
synagogue at Nazareth. Luke describes how Jesus found
the place in Isaiah to read from which said: 'The Spirit of
the Lord is on me, because he has anointed me to preach
good news to the poor. He has sent me to proclaim freedom
for the prisoners and recovery of sight for the blind, to
release the oppressed, to proclaim the year of the Lord's
favour.' He goes on to say how the eyes of everyone were
fastened on Jesus as He began to speak to them saying
'Today this scripture is fulfilled in your hearing' (Luke
4:18–20).

Even before this event, news of Jesus' teaching and
ministering had spread through the whole countryside.
Luke however wrote the account of Jesus in the synagogue at Nazareth ahead of any mention of Him speaking
about the kingdom of God. This soon follows (v43) but
Luke is hinting that the understanding of Jesus' mission
should be set first and foremost in seeing how Jesus
fulfilled that prophecy from Isaiah.

He had come with good news for the poor. He had come
to tell all those who were disenfranchised in any way,
that there was a gospel of liberation. Even without the
prophecy Jesus said He had come to fulfil, the way He
ministered the good news demonstrated what it meant
for individuals who recognized their poverty. What would
be less clear without the prologue Luke uses is that the

in-break of the kingdom was for more than just the restoration of individuals. It was that society itself might be restored. The anointing of the Spirit Jesus spoke of was that He could proclaim in word and deed the 'year of the Lord's favour'. This was to go far beyond the restoration of individuals – as far as the healing of nations.

To appreciate how vital the anointing of the Spirit is for preaching the 'year of the Lord's favour', the setting of that anointing in Isaiah 61:1–2 needs to be understood. It was that of the captivity of the people of Israel in Babylon. Into this situation was given a prophecy of both the deliverance from physical and spiritual bondage as well as the total restoration which God desired to give to them. The 'year of the Lord's favour' was particularly symbolic. It was a reference to the 'year of Jubilee' (described in Leviticus chapter 25) which God had commanded. Every seven years was to have been a 'sabbatical year' for the nation, when the land was allowed to rest. Every fiftieth year, that is after every seven sabbaticals, there was to be the year of Jubilee, when the trumpet was to be sounded to proclaim liberty throughout the land.

The year of Jubilee was the announcement of the restoration, or renewal of society. Slaves were to be set free and returned to their families. Property that had been sold was to revert to the original owners, and debts were to be cancelled. This special year was given not just to normalize the economic systems, but to prevent the entrenchment of the haves and the have-notes, the powerful and the powerless. It was to bring healing to the way the people lived together, such that dependency on God and His gracious providence was put back in its primary place.

There is little evidence however that it was practised – the demands of it exposed where the heart of the people lay. To these people now exiled in Babylon because of their continued turning from God, Isaiah prophesied the year of the Lord's favour. He was speaking of the reinstatement of what God had originally given to bring healing to the nation. It symbolized not just individual healing, but national healing, in which the renewing of society was of the highest value.

In saying He had been anointed by the Spirit to fulfil that prophecy, Jesus was doing two things. Firstly, He was describing the nature of the healing He had come to bring. It was not just for individuals in their poverty, crucial as that is, but for nations in their poverty of ability to live in harmony within, as well as between, themselves. Secondly, Jesus was identifying with Isaiah's prophecy of the Suffering Servant on whom God would put His Spirit to bring justice to the nations (Isaiah 42:1). It would be through Him that many nations would marvel, and kings would shut their mouths because of Him (Isaiah 52:15). He was the Suffering Servant who had come to inaugurate the kingdom of God, from the ground floor of healing individuals right up to healing the life of societies and nations. Even that which had become entrenched and unredressed through the generations was to be healed.

Luke's bringing to the fore of Jesus' rejection in Nazareth, was therefore very deliberate. It was intended to shape our understanding of the good news of the kingdom which Jesus had come to inaugurate, and which we are called to continue. Among other things, Luke invites us through it to go beyond an individualistic understanding of why the Spirit was given. He encourages us to see the anointing of the Spirit not as something to be privatized, but for our role as individuals in the healing of society, on which the healing of nations depends.

Jeremiah, Nehemiah and social mire

The role of individuals in God's purposes for the healing of the nations is in fact a theme developed across Scripture. It is typified by the story of what happened to Jeremiah when he went down to the potter's house. As he watched the potter working at his wheel, Jeremiah saw that the pot he was shaping was marred in his hands. The potter decided to form it into another pot, shaping it as seemed best to him.

Then God spoke to Jeremiah.

> 'O house of Israel, can I not do with you as this potter does? . . . Like clay in the hand of the potter, so are you in my hand, O house of Israel. If at any time I announce that a nation or kingdom is to be uprooted, torn down and destroyed, and if that nation I warned repents of its evil, then I will relent and not inflict on it the disaster I had planned. And if at another time I announce that a nation or kingdom is to be built up and planted, and if it does evil in my sight and does not obey me, then I will reconsider the good I had intended to do for it.'
>
> (Jeremiah 18:6–10)

Though God was speaking to Jeremiah of His sovereign power to build up or destroy nations, God had also previously spoken to him of the desire He has to accomplish His purposes for nations through individuals.

Earlier, when Jeremiah had questioned God's calling of him because of his youth, God said 'I have put my words in your mouth. See, today I appoint you over nations and kingdoms to uproot and tear down, to destroy and overthrow, to build and to plant' (Jeremiah 1:10).

God had specifically called Jeremiah to minister His word into the mire of Israel's society to affect what was at its very heart. He would base His choice of what to do with them on their response. God wanted to bring healing to the nation, or at least what was left of it, through that one man, despite his youth.

It was to be a very costly calling. As a result of his prophecy of the downfall of Jerusalem and the destruction of the Temple, Jeremiah was arrested, imprisoned, and thrown into a muddy cistern. It was only because of the empowering and envisioning he had received from

God that he was able to continue to reveal the way of
healing to the nation of Israel. They rejected God's word
to them through Jeremiah, and in consequence, it was
they, rather than he, who ended up in the real mire. They
were taken into exile, and Jerusalem was left in ruins.

God's heart never ceases to be for the healing of nations,
notwithstanding their rejection of Him. Even to a nation
that does not call on His name, God still says 'Here am
I, here am I' (Isaiah 65:1). In the due course of time, God
touched the heart of Nehemiah, and for him too it meant a
journey into hardship and threat that healing might once
more be offered to the nation of Israel. Again, it was only
because of the empowering and envisioning of God that
he was able to follow through what he had been called
to do.

Nehemiah had a comfortable position in life, as cup-
bearer to King Artaxerxes. However bad life was for
Israel, it was not bad for him. Yet when word came to
him of the state of Jerusalem he sat down and wept. The
remnant who had survived the exile were in great trouble
and disgrace. The wall of Jerusalem was broken down,
and its gates burned with fire. He mourned and fasted
and prayed (Nehemiah 1:4). He interceded for Israel,
confessing its sins as if they were his own, pleading with
God for His redemption of what had happened. He chose
to venture into the place of pain on behalf of the nation,
however costly the action might be.

Even the king saw how touched he was in his spirit.
Nehemiah asked for permission to visit Jerusalem, that
he might personally feel its pain. This he did. Nehemiah's
conviction was that the rebuilding of the wall should be
commenced straight away. At once he faced mockery and
derision (2:19). As the building progressed he faced the
anger of his enemies who threatened to come and fight
against them, to cause trouble, indeed to come and kill
them (4:7–11). Nehemiah's life was then threatened
(6:11). On top of this there was the discouragement of
the people to contend with when faced with the size of

the task. It was all a very long way from the comforts of the royal court. Yet the rebuilding of the wall was completed and when Nehemiah's enemies and the surrounding nations saw it, they lost their self-confidence, because they realized this work had been done with 'the help of our God' (6:16). Furthermore, the people returned to Jerusalem, and a time of spiritual renewal followed when the Law was again read, and the Feast of Tabernacles reinstated.

Though it is an exciting account, it only came about because of Nehemiah's willingness to deny himself comfort, and to go into the place of suffering and potential death. What he and Jeremiah had exposed themselves to was the loss of their physical wellbeing that healing might come to a nation. As Isaiah wrote, it is one thing to fast privately for a nation, another to engage with the true fast God has called us to.

'Is not this the kind of fasting I have chosen:
to loose the chains of injustice
    and untie the cords of the yoke,
to set the oppressed free
    and break every yoke?
Is it not to share your food with the hungry
    and to provide the poor wanderer with shelter –
when you see the naked, to clothe him,
    and not to turn away from your own flesh and
        blood?
Then your light will break forth like the dawn,
    and your healing will quickly appear;
then your righteousness will go before you,
    and the glory of the Lord will be your rear guard.
Then you will call, and the Lord will answer;
    you will cry for help, and he will say: Here am I.
If you do away with the yoke of oppression,
    with the pointing finger and malicious talk,
and if you spend yourselves on behalf of the hungry
    and satisfy the needs of the oppressed,

then your light will rise in the darkness,
    and your night will become like the noonday.
The Lord will guide you always;
    he will satisfy your needs in a
        sun-scorched land
    and will strengthen your frame.
You will be like a well-watered garden,
    like a spring whose waters never fail.
Your people will rebuild the ancient ruins
    and will raise up the age-old foundations;
you will be called Repairer of Broken Walls,
    Restorer of Streets with Dwellings'. (Isaiah 58:6–12)

When Jesus stood up on the last day of the Feast of Tabernacles to speak of streams of living water flowing from those who come to drink of Him, He was speaking of the equipping of Spirit-filled believers to live out the fast of Isaiah. Though the Spirit delights to bless and heal those whom He fills, it is not for their increased comfort, but that they may be equipped and released to go into the place of discomfort that such things as injustice and oppression may be tackled, that the starving may be fed and the homeless cared for. By themselves such actions do not restore a nation, just as the rebuilding of the walls of Jerusalem did not spiritually restore Israel. What they do provide, however, as the renewed walls of Jerusalem provided, is the milieu in which the spiritual heart of a nation can be lifted out of the mire and revived.

The final healing of the nations will not happen until the fullness of the river flows from the throne, but the streams we have at present still have the mighty power of God to build up or destroy entire societies and nations. However exciting spiritual gifts may be in personal experience, their ultimate purpose is not for spiritual self-interest. The real blessing is to be found not by a privatized keeping of that living water for ourselves, but by a more public pouring out of it on to a spiritually sun-scorched land, for the revival and restoration only God can bring about.

Such ministry of healing will have neither the clean-handed, superficial excitement, nor the safety, of the four walls of charismatic meetings. Indeed, as those worshippers in Leningrad knew, it is not only costly, but can seem so inconsequential. Yet what they were to discover was that even the name of their city would be changed within two decades. What God wants us also to discover is that He has capacity to bring about healing in any and every nation, which is immeasurably more than all we might think or imagine. He wants us to lift our eyes to the pinnacle of His healing purposes. The healing of individuals is nothing more than the ground-floor. We have no choice but to use it as the way in. Yet the longer we just stay there, the more privatized our view of the healing ministry is likely to become. A mature model of healing must therefore show the way up.

13

How Is Society Healed?

For some years revival has been talked about as being imminent. Compared with where the church has been, it may seem that we are on the fringes of it. Yet honest assessment can only describe what we presently have as renewal rather than revival. Revival is when the heart of a nation is touched. Some would suggest we are just a few short steps from it. Others would suggest that some very giant leaps are still needed. The determining factor seems to be the degree of confidence, or otherwise, in a sufficient presence of the gifts of the Spirit to bring it about.

I was once asked 'If you were a Martian looking in on the world, and you saw a healing conference in every major city of the world whilst the Third World went unfed, would they cause you to worship Jesus Christ?' It pinpointed the issue. How can a society be healed? Present experience of lack of progress towards revival suggests that no amount of charismatic giftedness, kept to itself by the church, will bring healing to the heart of a nation. A more mature model of healing is therefore needed, one which demonstrates to a sceptical world not only the healing of individuals, but how healing of a higher order is ministered, which touches the ailments of the society in which we live.

There is only one thing that Scripture describes which will in practice make the difference between renewal within the church, and revival that affects the spiritual state of the nation. It is the ministering of the type of healing which reflects the 'year of the Lord's favour'. Deeds as well as words are needed to express how it is God's way to heal the injustices of society.

Unfortunately, human determination to make it happen will not be enough. We are no more likely to succeed at it in our own strength than the people of Israel were. It requires the power of the Spirit, and it depends on the heart of the church as to whether we are open to what receiving such power involves. It would involve a fundamental reorientation from the selfish consumption of blessing, both material and spiritual, to a primary commitment to the giving away of it. It would certainly mean a foregoing of comfort, as well as the letting go of pre-occupation with their own need for healing that stops many from being available to God in the way they might be.

So it is not the scale of our praise meetings, but the scale of our willingness to lay down our lives under the anointing and the motivation of the Spirit that will make the difference. The tough question we therefore need to face concerns what is lacking in us in terms of the willingness that is needed. Part of the answer is obviously to do with how a heart for holiness is established. However, there may well be another part to it, which is to do with our lack of conviction that God's heart is not only for the redemption of individuals, but indeed for the whole of creation itself.

God's heart for the redemption of individuals, expressed through the Holy Spirit's presence within us, is something we are very familiar with. Paul writes: 'We ourselves, who have the firstfruits of the Spirit, groan inwardly as we wait eagerly for our adoption as sons, the redemption of our bodies' (Romans 8:23).

Yet far less notice is taken of the mention of this same 'groaning' also being manifested in creation:

The creation waits in eager expectation for the sons of God to be revealed. For the creation was subjected

to frustration, not by its own choice, but by the will
of the one who subjected it, in hope that the creation
itself will be liberated from its bondage to decay and
brought into the glorious freedom of the children of
God. (Romans 8:19–21)

Mark Stibbe[1] has pointed out that the reason why both
Christian and creation are the locus for the same yearning for liberation is because the same Spirit is at work in
both. He has argued the case for a charismatic theology
of creation because

... it is the Spirit of God who is the link between
creation and Creator. It is the Spirit of God who
is the link between creation and the Christian. In
the final analysis, any pneumatology or doctrine of
the Holy Spirit which is purely concerned with the
work of the Spirit in the church, or, worse still, in
us as individual Christians, is hopelessly myopic.
The Holy Spirit is concerned not only with our
own liberation, but also the liberation of societies,
cultures, nature and indeed the whole cosmos.
(See figure 1)

The full span of God's heart for redemption is from the
individual to the cosmos, embracing everything that that
includes. Ultimately it will be a different form of redemption for the cosmos than for the individual, because there
is going to be a new heaven and a new earth (Revelation
21:1). Yet that will only happen after Jesus Christ has
first physically returned to this earth. There would be
no need for such a physical return were it not for God's
heart for the healing of the earth that presently exists. It
would be possible for justice to be meted out to the living
and the dead without the physical return of the Judge to
this earth. Thus there must be an outworking of justice
which only His return to this earth can satisfy, which is
to do with the restoration of creation itself.

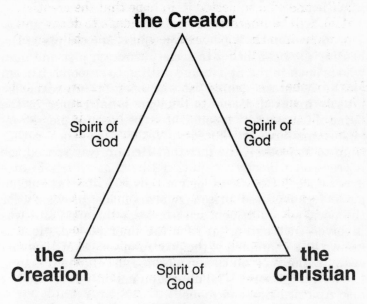

Figure 1.

The present charismatic movement has yet to address this in any significant measure, and therefore has developed little faith for how God can minister healing through the church not just to individuals, but to society, and to the environment. We are therefore leaving the way wide open to the New Age movement to insidiously fill the vacuum through our ignoring of the warning by Paul about the vulnerability of people to 'turn their ears away from truth and turn aside to myths' (2 Timothy 4:4). It will be no more than a spurious healing of society and creation that the New Age movement will offer, but in the absence of anything more authentic, it may come to look deceptively attractive. Yet we are not without example from earlier generations of how healing can be ministered to society in the context of revival and even through single individuals.

The potential of one man for the healing of society

The story of John Wesley is an amazing example of the
healing God can bring to society through just one man
who is open to the Spirit, and willing to respond. Known
as the itinerant evangelist and open-air preacher, he
greatly inspired people to take up social causes in the
name of Christ, which penetrated the heart of the nation.
Historians have attributed to Wesley's influence, rather
than to any other, the fact that Britain was spared the
horrors of a bloody revolution like that which France
experienced. He was a prime mover in the attack on
slavery, advocated prison reform, made provision for
the poor, set up dispensaries to treat the sick, and was
involved in creating jobs for the unemployed. He was
known as a champion of the poor man's point of view and
set in motion a revolution in morals and behaviour among
the working classes. The impact on not only England but
also America was enormous.

Yet the faith of the man who said 'I look upon the
world as my parish' began in a very personal way when
on 24th May, 1738, his heart was 'strangely warmed'.
He recorded in his journal his subsequent charismatic
experience on 1st January, 1739 when,

> About three in the morning, as we were continuing
> instant in prayer, the power of God came mightily
> upon us insomuch as that many cried out for exceed-
> ing joy and many fell to the ground. As soon as we
> were recovered a little from that awe and amazement
> at the presence of His majesty, we broke out with one
> voice 'We praise Thee, O God, we acknowledge Thee
> to be the Lord'.

Many today whose personal experience of God has been
enlarged by charismatic experience want, like Wesley, to

share their faith – albeit perhaps not on quite his scale!
Far fewer see as Wesley did the relationship between the
gospel and society. Healing of body and spirit is seen as for
individuals rather than for the nation, however desperate
its need. One wonders, however, what a modern day
John Wesley, who understood how God can multiply the
consequence of one person's efforts, might be used of God
to accomplish.

Stanley Baldwin, the former Tory Prime Minister,
made a speech on February 11th, 1926 about exactly
this, saying:

> Many people, I fear, today fail to realize the very
> critical period through which the country is passing.
> There is nothing the country so needs as another
> Wesley or Whitfield. Those spiritual movements,
> such as occurred in the Eighteenth century, led
> largely by Wesley, have come from time to time in
> the history of the human race. Their spirit is always
> the same, though their form is different. Had Wesley
> been born four centuries earlier, he would have been
> Wesley just the same, but he would have worn a
> rough robe girded with a cord and have founded a
> great body of preaching friars. I confess I am not
> sure, if a Wesley or a St Francis arose today, that
> to found a body of preaching friars would not be the
> best they could do for the world.[2]

Baldwin begs the question of what approach a Wesley of
today would take. It would be very different from that for
which he is remembered, but the principle would be the
same. He would be looking for how, under the anointing
of the Spirit, God desires to bring healing to the nation
even through just one man. 'Given one hundred,' Wesley
once said 'who fear nothing but sin and desire nothing but
God, and I care not a straw whether they be clergymen or
laymen, such alone will shake the gates of hell and set up
the kingdom of God on earth.' Such was his vision of how

God can use individuals for the healing and revival of a
nation through the combination of evangelism and social
action.

Despite the feeling that revival is within reach, and
despite our experience of the Spirit, there is little evidence
to date of such Wesleyan type vision for the healing of
our nation. So far the church does not seem to have
been permeated by Luke's message that it is the same
anointing of the Holy Spirit for the proclamation of
the year of the Lord's favour as it is for charismatic
phenomena. The challenge of Wesley is to see how in
our modern times the dual anointing of the Spirit may
be received, that our nation may be impacted with both
spiritual and social healing.

Where to begin?

Evangelist as he was, Wesley saw through the premise
that revival can only ever begin through the changing
of the hearts of individuals. The argument would seem
logical that slum clearance has to take place in people's
hearts before it can take place in their homes. To reverse
the process merely produces sinners who are also comfortable and educated. However, as the experience of South
Africa and Northern Ireland currently demonstrates,
extensive preaching of individual conversion can still
leave nations in extreme need of healing.[3] The reason
is that it is not the individual, but relationships which
are at the heart of society, and it is these which also have
to be touched in order for healing to come to a nation.

Richard Lovelace, in *Dynamics of Spiritual Life* puts it
this way.

> Many believers conclude from reading the New Tes-
> tament that the shortest route to social change is
> changing hearts through preaching the gospel and
> making disciples through 'spiritual instruction', so
> that our main duty to the poor is to preach the

gospel to them. I believe this conclusion is natural, but wrong, for reasons which can be clearly identified both in Scripture and history. First the Old Testament shows that whenever professing believers become so dominant in a society that they can influence its structures, they are responsible to help establish justice.

He continues to say

If we only had Matthew 25:31–46 and the letter of James, we would have to conclude that the New Testament is as uncompromisingly earthy and literal as the Old in its demands for social justice. It calls for sacrifices which are not payable only in spiritual and emotional currency. They cost money and effort as well as love.[4]

His argument, part of his 'unified field theory of spirituality' is that the healing of nations happens only as the change of individuals through the gospel is coupled to the bringing about of justice through social action. Complicated as it sounds, this is exactly what Wesley got on with in order to begin an authentic revival. Most importantly, it is what Jesus modelled. He not only proclaimed through His reference to the 'year of the Lord's favour' that He would do it, but the comment in retrospect on His ministry was that He did do it.

Under the anointing of the Holy Spirit, 'He went around doing good and healing all who were under the power of the devil' (Acts 10:38). There was a dual aspect to His ministry. He not only healed individuals, but did good by putting His finger on the ways the society of His day needed healing. If we are to 'obey everything' He has commanded, then to omit this aspect of the great commission is to be selective about both the anointing of the Holy Spirit and our response to what Jesus commanded.

Social change is going on around us all the time. To do nothing whatsoever about the society which surrounds us, if only by default, makes us accomplices to change which causes increasing hurt and harm. As Edmund Burke said 'The only thing necessary for the triumph of evil is for good men to do nothing.' If our heart is for revival, then there is a positive imperative not just to pray 'Your kingdom come', but to take steps which contribute to it in practice. As David Sheppard wrote in *Built as a City* 'If we believe that God's future kingdom will have justice and peace as features of its life, it is a powerful argument to work with all our strength to bring those features into action now.'[5]

The fact that the depth of society's need for healing is so enormous is no reason not to seek to minister healing to it. The enormity of the nation's physical ill-health does not stop us from praying for people where we can. As a result, faith for personal healing has mushroomed in just a few years. The pictures of Wesley, and so many others, should encourage us in relation to ministering healing to our nation. They demonstrate God's desire and ability to multiply the actions of one individual out of all proportion to this end. He has made us the salt of the earth, to be as salt which affects what it flavours out of all proportion to its size. So we may have vision to affect our nation as we touch it with the proclamation of the year of the Lord's favour, starting right where we are.

Heart for the City

A heart for the social health of where we live is not always a characteristic of the local church. Sometimes this is dismissed by the super spiritual on the basis that we are just passing through, like Abraham who was 'looking forward to the city with foundations, whose architect and builder is God' (Hebrews 11:10). Yet God's word to the people of Israel even when they were in exile was still very clear. It was to 'seek the peace and prosperity of the city to which I have carried you into exile. Pray to the Lord for it, because if it prospers, you too will prosper' (Jeremiah 29:7).

This is not the prosperity gospel prayer which focuses on individual wellbeing regardless of how well others are doing. It is about the welfare of all involved in the network of relationships where we live, whether or not they directly concern us. Their importance is highlighted by the reference to the word 'city' or 'cities' over 1200 times in Scripture. They were not so much defined by their size as by their character, which was as guarded places in which people dwelt. It is the sense of spiritual guarding that the Church needs to rediscover.

The heart of Jesus was profoundly touched over the city of Jerusalem. 'O Jerusalem, Jerusalem, you who kill the prophets and stone those sent to you, how often I have longed to gather your children together, as a hen gathers her chicks under her wings, but you were not willing. Look, your house is left to you desolate' (Matthew 23:37–38). At that stage Jerusalem appeared anything other than desolate: its destruction was not to take place for another forty years. Yet Jesus saw the spiritual state of the earthly city that had rejected Him and grieved deeply for it. If our desire is to minister healing out of the compassion of Jesus, then it has to include a heart for the healing of what underlies the temporal places we live and work in. Given the prediction that by AD 2000 for the first time in human history 50 per cent of all the world's peoples will live in cities,[6] the role of Christian witness and influence in the temporal places we live and work in is becoming increasingly vital. This is where our personal part in the healing of the nation is to be expressed.

The question is how to exercise Christian social action which is different from purely humanitarian action, and which reflects the year of the Lord's favour. The answer is to look at the pattern Jesus gave, which was of power through weakness, of willingness to wash the disciples feet. John 13:12–17 offers a most important picture of how healing can be ministered not just to individuals, but to the very heart of the society where we live.

> When he had finished washing their feet, he put on his clothes and returned to his place. 'Do you understand what I have done for you?' he asked them. 'You call me 'Teacher' and 'Lord', and rightly so, for that is what I am. Now that I, your Lord and Teacher, have washed your feet, you also should wash one another's feet. I have set you an example that you should do as I have done for you. I tell you the truth, no servant is greater than his master, nor is a messenger greater than the one who sent him. Now that you know these things, you will be blessed if you do them.

For us to be the channels of God's healing into the place where we live, it requires no more than a desire to feel the grief of God over the pain of what underlies the superficial appearances, and a willingness to follow after the Suffering Servant, acting in His name. It requires no more, but no less. The example of Mother Teresa of Calcutta demonstrated God's power to multiply out of all proportion the impact of those who are willing to wash the feet of others in Jesus' name. From a human angle, the likelihood of this one physically-diminutive woman having any effect on her nation, let alone upon the world, was minimal. To do it through the rescuing of dying people from the gutters and rubbish tips where they had been left, simply in order to give them a dignified death, is even more improbable. Yet through her obedience to seek the welfare of the city in which God had placed her, people in many nations have been touched by her example.

Here is present-day illustration of the proclamation of the acceptable year of the Lord. It reflects God's love in giving His one and only Son, not just for the church, but for the healing of the world and the whole of creation.

It reflects the willingness to get our hands sacrificially dirtied with the world, as God did through Jesus. It reflects faith which knows in personal experience the reality of resurrection life that has power to meet us in the darkest valley, to bring healing from the 'bottom up', indeed to bring good out of evil. In this lies the route to the fullness of revival, which comes when healing is ministered not just to individuals but to the very wounds of a society and a nation as we see them, right where we live.

The invitation to aspire to such illustration inevitably seems like being asked to jump a staircase in one go. What is needed in a mature model of healing is insight as to how we may go up one step at a time. To this we now turn.

14

What Do We Do When We Fail In Healing?

During the firemen's strike of 1978, the Army took over the emergency fire-fighting and rescue service. A call from an elderly lady in South London to retrieve her cat which had become trapped up a tree was to leave an indelible mark on the memories of all those who went to its aid. They arrived with great haste and quickly did what was necessary. The old lady was so grateful she invited them all in for tea. Driving off later, bidding fond farewells, they ran over the cat![1]

Learning to minister healing has its unexpected hazards as well. However enthusiastic our response to a call for help, there is simply no guarantee of what will happen. The more obvious pitfalls can be avoided. What cannot be avoided however is the reality of the gap between vision for healing and what actually happens. The inescapable fact of the healing ministry is that no one, not even the most up-front televangelist, claims 100 percent success. The tough question this poses for all who would seek to mature in the ministry of healing is how, with integrity, to sustain the ministry when inevitably we fail and get it wrong?

Frequently Paul's words will come back to us – 'who is equal to such a task?' (2 Corinthians 2:16). There will be times when we will look at where we are and wonder what it will take to get to where we want to be. Like the Irishman, who when asked by an Englishman the way to Dublin replied, 'If that's where you're wanting to go, I wouldn't start from here!' We may conclude it

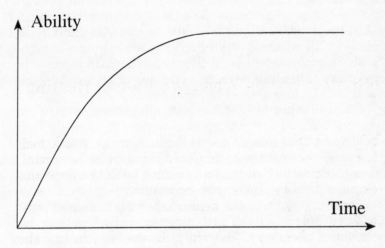

Fig. One

might be better if we were starting from somewhere else. Unfortunately though we can only go from where we are. What understanding then should a mature model of healing express about the learning process that those who minister healing will always be involved in?

Learning anything can be a mixture of excitement and frustration where the sort of support we receive can be a big factor in how well we cope. A toddler learning to walk can get tremendous encouragement from his onlookers. He may wobble forwards and backwards between steps, but they cheer him on regardless of how many falls result. By contrast, a learner driver who holds up the traffic and scratches the sides of parked cars doesn't receive quite such enthusiastic support! Learning new things may or may not be enjoyable. However, the process for learning almost all things in life, healing included, is described by the 'learning curve' (see figure 1) which shows the improvement of ability with practice.

Ability begins at zero, improving as what has been

learnt is put into practice. The law of diminishing returns applies, such that progress gets less rapid as time goes on, and eventually plateaus. The timescale depends on the skill involved. Walking is a skill we can plateau in quite early in life whereas driving a car is something where the plateau comes later in life. Other skills, which include the ministry of healing, we can keep going at all our days and will still be learning at the end.

What it takes to push towards a learning plateau can vary greatly. Some things can be learnt entirely from books, and the risk of doing much damage to others in the process is not too high. Other things, like learning to drive, ultimately hinge on practice, with the hope that damage done to others may be minimal!

Learning to minister healing, however we may wish it were not, is in the latter category rather than the former. There is no substitute for doing it in practice, and for living with the consequences of three things. Firstly, the gap that is there for all who are involved in the healing ministry. Secondly, the consequences of our lack of expertise. Thirdly, the opposition of the evil one who has no desire for us to learn about it.

However much support we get and whatever early breakthroughs we have in ministering healing, it will not be long before we face real discouragement in 'learning by doing'. It is at this stage we need to understand not just the idealized learning curve for healing, but what the realistic expectation of it is. Far from a smooth pattern of progress, it is a series of peaks and troughs superimposed on an upward trend (see figure 2).

The 'up and down' roller-coaster experience of learning about healing can cause us to get stuck in a variety of ways (see figure 3). Cautiousness may result in the attempt to stick with a short-term peak, so constraining the situation that nothing more or less can happen (Route A). This is what some churches would appear to be trying to do at present. The positive side of this is that it ensures that what has been secured will not nose-dive, at least in

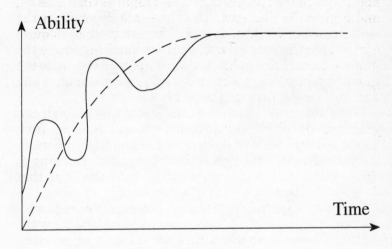

Fig. Two

the short-term. However, the good can be the enemy of the
best, which needs a willingness to press forwards through
all the ups and downs of learning new things by exploring
new avenues of healing.

Where more churches would seem to be getting stuck
is at the bottom of a trough (Route B). Earlier experience
has seen greater heights, but the growing residue of
unresolved issues has led to a levelling-out well below
where they have been. It is not a freefall nose-dive that
some have found themselves in, eventually snuffing out
all that has been (Route C), but it would still require
something quite major to restart the learning process.
Compared with the first flush of excitement, the legacy of
disillusionment, and the new emphasis on caution, makes
a new start much more difficult.

For the long-term journey to be travelled in the healing
ministry (Route D), it is vital to be able to interpret the
trough experiences in the light of the learning curve.
This means that there will be times in the process of

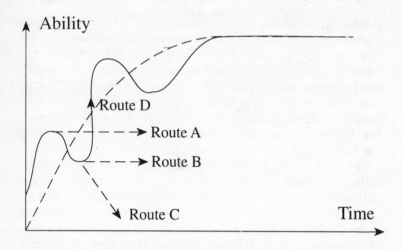

Fig. Three

pressing forwards when things will seem less good than
they were, but this is no reason to hold back. What is
going on is similar to the motion of the waves on the
seashore as the tide comes in. High tide can only be
reached through the waves coming in and going out,
each time a little further up the shore until high tide is
reached. However the power of the undertow as a wave
goes back out before another comes in can make it hard
to tell which way things are really flowing. Only in time,
rather than in the moment, can the fullness of the tide
be seen.

Staying with the learning curve of healing will inevitably involve times when the undertow has simply got to
be stood against, even though it feels as if things are going
the wrong way. It is certainly possible to step out of it and
to go our own route. However to do so is to opt out of what
is dynamic, and to step into what is at best static but at
worst stagnant, which is the antithesis of the life-giving
nature of healing.

The disciples' learning curve for healing

Whilst the learning curve is a modern-day concept, Jesus introduced the disciples to the reality of it as they learnt how to minister healing. He prepared them for the experience of failure and rejection, as well as for the need of on-going commitment to keep pressing forwards into new things. This is graphically described in Luke chapter 9, the account of how the Twelve were first sent out. Far from being an account of unbridled success, it is the honest account of hard lessons and stern rebukes.

The first lesson began with thrilling, good news. Jesus called the Twelve together (v1) to give them power and authority to drive out all demons and to cure diseases. Their excitement at the prospect of one day being able to heal like Jesus is not hard to imagine. Then came the bad news – you start right now! Doubtless Benjamin Disraeli's words would have meant much to them had he been there – 'It's much easier to be critical than correct!' Their role had suddenly changed from critical observers to up-front performers, out on their own. Things then turned from bad to worse. Jesus told them to 'take nothing for the journey – no staff, no bag, no bread, no money, no extra tunic' (v3). Which the greatest deprivation was is hard to guess – perhaps the lack of a spare tunic considering how some of them must have been sweating! Matthew adds Jesus' words (Matthew 10:16) that they were being sent out 'as sheep amongst wolves' emphasising the risk they were entering into. Out they went (v6), probably with hands shaking more out of fear than the power of the Spirit.

Yet they were able to come back with reports of healing people everywhere (v10). It worked! Wild excitement as they exchanged stories. It was the first stage up the learning curve, the phase of quickest progress. Unfortunately for them, what follows for the toddler after those first successful steps, followed for them – a fall flat on their faces.

Lesson Two happened during what is known as the story of Jesus feeding the five thousand. Immediately after telling Jesus what had happened on their tour of healing, they withdrew with Him to Bethsaida, but the crowds learned about it, and followed (v11). Jesus however welcomed them, taught them about the kingdom, and healed those who needed healing. Late on in the afternoon, the disciples came suggesting He should send the crowd away to find food and lodging because of the remoteness of where they were. Jesus' reply shocked them – 'You give them something to eat' (v13). Despite the miracles they had seen happen through their hands when they went out before, apparently they had no faith for what could happen in this situation, and Jesus had exposed it. Their earlier jubilation vaporised. All they could find was five loaves and two fishes, and their only idea was a mammoth shopping trip (v13).

The lesson Jesus taught them was vital for their future ministry of healing, as it is for all who minister – the most we will ever have in our hands to offer is a few crumbs. Jesus told the disciples to sit the crowd down in groups of fifty, and He blessed the tiny amount of food there was. A common understanding of what happened next was that the multiplication took place in Jesus' hands, and that all the disciples had to do was to take it out to the waiting crowd. The more likely explanation is that each was given the equivalent of half a loaf and a tiny piece of fish, and had to set off with just this. They must have died five thousand deaths in those few yards between Jesus and their first group of fifty hungry mouths.

Yet the multiplication did happen, not in Jesus' hands, but in theirs. First there was enough for a second person, then a third and so on. Not only was there enough for the whole of the first fifty, but there was some left over to start the second fifty, and then the third fifty, and so on such that all ate their fill, and twelve basketfuls of broken pieces were left over. As they saw how the crumbs Jesus had blessed were multiplied in their hands, they were back up at the top of the class again! Only, that is, to find that they were soon back down to the bottom again.

For Lesson Three we have to turn to Mark chapter 6 to see the story included directly after the feeding of the five thousand. After Jesus had dismissed the crowd, He made the disciples get in a boat and go on ahead of Him to Bethsaida, whilst He went up on a mountain to pray (vv45–46). The story tells of how the wind was strong and the disciples had to strain against the oars. Suddenly they saw Jesus walking on the lake, but thought He was a ghost. They were terrified (vv49–50). He spoke to them saying 'Take courage! It is I. Don't be afraid.' As Jesus climbed into the boat with them, the wind died down, and Mark comments that 'they were completely amazed, for they had not understood about the loaves; their hearts were hardened' (vv51–52). They were blind to the presence of the supernatural in their midst as their eyes were fixed on their personal struggle with adverse circumstances.

It had been a roller-coaster of ups and downs for the disciples as they learnt how to translate previous experiences of God's supernatural moving into a new set of circumstances. That, though, was not all they had to learn about. Luke goes on to relate even bigger ups and downs for them as they worked through the rebukes meted out to them by Jesus.

Rebuke Number One arose from their inability to heal a child. Apparently the disciples had tried to heal him of his convulsions, but had failed. Jesus rebuked them. 'O unbelieving and perverse generation . . . how long shall I stay with you and put up with you?' (Luke 9:41). Jesus then healed the boy. Apparently harsh words, but lack of faith and presence of sin had to be dealt with if progress was to be made in the ministry of healing.

Quite undaunted by this, an argument rapidly arose between them as to which of them was the greatest. It's not hard to imagine Peter saying 'Well I'm the only one who's walked on water . . .' and others replying

'. . . but you needed a lifebelt to be thrown to you!',
rolling around laughing as they did so. Then Peter
having another go saying 'Well, I was the one who
got the huge miraculous catch of fish . . .' and the
others mocking as they replied '. . . but it split your
nets and nearly sank your boat!' So the argument went
on, eventually precipitating Rebuke Number Two. Jesus
placed a little child amongst them and said 'Whoever
welcomes this little child in my name welcomes me . . .'
(v48). In the midst of their arrogance, Jesus used the
most compelling visual aid of humility. His finger pinpointed the need for their pride to be dealt with before
they could enter into being used to minister substantial
healing.

Despite the power of this second rebuke which must
have cut the disciples to the core, their very next words
precipitated Rebuke Number Three. As if to change the
subject John turned to Jesus and said 'Master, we saw
a man driving out demons in your name and we tried to
stop him, because he is not one of us.' What was meant
to quell the embarassment of the previous rebukes led
to yet another as Jesus responded 'Do not stop him, for
whoever is not against you is for you' (v50). They were
being elitist, and Jesus put His finger on the need to deal
with such superiority.

Rebuke Number Four is found just verses later. Jesus
had sent messengers on ahead to a Samaritan village to
get things ready for Him. The Samaritans had a bitter
feud with the Jews, such that they would not help anyone
on their journey to Jerusalem. It was clear that this was
the direction Jesus was heading, and so they didn't
welcome Him. James' and John's passing suggestion
was to call fire down and destroy them! Luke's use of
understatement in saying that Jesus simply turned and
rebuked them (v55) belies the depth of impact that Jesus'
words must have had on them.

Given that Luke was the 'beloved physician' (Colossians
4:14, RSV), the construction of this passage, which is

so much more distinctively pointed than its other Gospel parallels, needs to be noted. Through it Luke was evidently making a diagnosis. In the most caring and sensitive way, he was presenting the truth of the condition the disciples were in when they began as learners in the healing ministry. Through it he also encourages us to recognize the condition from which we have to move forwards as we press on in the journey of learning about healing.

Luke's message about learning

Though Luke is paving the way for us to see the extent of the treatment we need, he is also paving the way to encourage us. We need to remember that Luke's Gospel was only volume one of the two-part volume he wrote. In volume two, the Acts of the Apostles, he developed the story of how the disciples continued the ministry of Jesus, including the ministry of many remarkable healings. Having been so forthright about the disciples' starting point, Luke delights to show how much better they became at it.

His message was to encourage those who with much goodwill venture into the ministry of healing, only to find themselves, as a result of it, facing hard lessons and rebukes which expose the weakness of their character. In his gentleness, Luke prepares us for the realities of the learning curve for healing. There is no short cut for the treatment of our basic condition. Yet he encourages us to see that, given the commitment to live as learners, whatever the apparent failures along the way, amazing progress is possible.

Behind all that Luke describes in his ninth chapter about what the disciples got wrong, he also invites us to see what they got right. Despite each of the troughs, they had stayed with it. In our language, they were committed to Route D! They may have been in panic when they were sent out as 'sheep amongst wolves', but at least they

went. They may not have understood about the feeding
of the five thousand, but at least they did it. They may
have failed to heal the demonized boy, but at least they
tried. They may have argued over who was the greatest,
but at least they aspired to greatness in the kingdom
of God. They may have wrongly condemned a man for
casting out a demon in Jesus' name, but at least they
cared. They may have been wrong to want to call down
fire from heaven on the Samaritans, but at least they
had faith that it was possible. What they got right in
amongst all their errors was the need to persevere, and
it was this that enabled them to move forwards on the
learning curve of healing.

Though the apostles were subsequently venerated,
what they were like as learners needs to be remembered.
At this stage they were still very much the men Jesus
had selected after His night praying (Luke 6:12–16).
They were neither educated, nor of social standing,
let alone spiritual giants. In fact they were a motley
group to entrust the advancement of the kingdom of God
to. Simon, whom Jesus named Peter, was impetuous.
Matthew, the tax-gatherer, was a quisling who had sold
himself to the Romans for personal gain. Simon, who
was called the Zealot, was a firebrand, a nationalist
amongst nationalists. To James and John, Jesus gave the
name Boanerges, which means Sons of Thunder. Iscariot
could have meant 'dagger-man', the ancient equivalent of
'gun-man'. Thomas was later to be seen as the doubter,
and so on. These were not innately gifted men, but simply
those Jesus called to be His disciples – the word literally
meaning 'learners'. Their only qualification was their
willingness to persevere at learning.

Indeed central to their call to be disciples was the
tackling by Jesus of the points at which they thought they
did have personal strength. Jesus' call of Peter, James
and John, (Luke 5:11) came after a night's unsuccessful
fishing. It was only with the greatest reluctance that
Peter was willing to obey Jesus and put out into the

deep water to let down the nets once more. If there was anything Peter knew about, it was when and how to fish on the Sea of Galilee. Yet in doing so the catch of fish was so large that their nets began to break and not just Peter's boat but even their partner's other boat began to sink. He and his companions were astonished at the size of the catch. Peter's pride was broken as he was caused to recognize that Jesus is indeed the Master in every area, from whom he had to learn.

Such is the process of learning for all who would be disciples of Jesus. His supernatural power flows through us only insofar as we have been broken at what we regard as our points of strength. God can only truly use those who are weak. Perseverance in learning is therefore not about our competence to learn from Jesus, but about recognizing the ongoing need to do so. It is this which is the basis of genuine willingness. Thus we should not be surprised when we find the areas of our lives where we think we know best being fundamentally challenged, that we might learn more of Him.

Ultimately, it is the shaping of who we are in our being which is most crucial to our availability to God to learn what we need to. His permission of adverse circumstances to expose how we need to be touched by Him is something we therefore need to anticipate. Luke's brief account of the disciple's encounter with the storm (8:22–25) describes this to a tee.

Jesus had suggested that they cross the lake: it was a situation He had invited them into. As they sailed, He fell asleep, and a squall came down on the lake so that the boat was being swamped and they were in great danger. Considering that at least some of them had much experience of the lake, the disciples' reaction of fear that they thought they were going to die meant it was an extreme situation they were in. It felt out of control, and Jesus, still asleep, didn't even seem to care. Yet after they had woken Him and He had rebuked the wind and the raging waters so that all became calm, it was their turn to be rebuked. 'Where is your faith?' he asked. Their faith had been in their ability to navigate the storm. Their faith was in themselves. For them to navigate the storms which would lie ahead, faith in their own competence had to be replaced with faith in Him. There was no substitute for such experiences for learning about faith in the One who was in the boat with them. So it is also for us.

This then is the perspective for the second half of the story Luke tells, in the Acts of the Apostles. In it are the accounts of the healing ministry after Jesus was no longer physically present with them. They had arisen from a newly-found lifestyle of learning about the difference that faith in Jesus makes for doing His works. Yet they are centred in the lives of those who had no natural giftedness for the journey of learning. They are designed to give hope to everyone who will keep persevering through all the ups and downs, recognizing that there are no quick and easy ways through the tough lessons which need to be learnt.

An important feature of the way Luke writes up some of the stories of healing in Acts is the striking parallel they have with those of Jesus recorded in the Gospels. It is not that Luke is saying that they had discovered a formula for healing, but simply that they were committed to living out to the full what they had learnt from Jesus.

For example, the healing of the lame man in Acts chapter 3 and of Aeneas in Acts chapter 9 bears remarkable resemblance to the healing of the paralytic in Luke chapter 5. To the paralytic Jesus gave three commands. 'Get up, take your mat, and go home.' Each of those words were 'go on and do it' instructions that Jesus initiated, but that the man had to choose to complete, which he did. In Acts chapter 3, Peter similarly instructs the man to walk, initiates it by taking him by the hand to help him up, but leaves it to the man to go on and complete the healing, which he did. (vv7–8). In Acts chapter 9, Peter tells Aeneas, a paralytic who had been bedridden for eight years, to get up and tidy up his mat. Again, healing initiated by Peter, but which required Aeneas to go on and complete, which he did.

Another direct comparison is that of the raising of Dorcas in Acts chapter 9 with the raising of Jairus' daughter in Luke chapter 8. When he arrived at the house of Jairus, Jesus put everyone else outside, except Peter, James and John, and the child's father and mother. He then took the girl by the hand, telling her to get up. At once she stood up (v53). The healing of Dorcas is almost like a television remake. When Peter arrived, he put the mourners outside, then told the dead woman to get up. She opened her eyes, and sat up. He took her by the hand and helped her to her feet (v40).

The healing of Publius' father by Paul in Acts chapter 28 also has a parallel with the healing of Peter's mother-in-law in Luke chapter 4. Details vary, but the principle is the same. By this stage, Luke's account has become broadened far beyond the original disciples and their personal experience of the learning curve for healing. It now embraces Paul. Like the other disciples he also had to be broken at what he regarded as his strong points in order to learn how to do the works of Jesus. Yet through him and all those who were willing to persevere, came a witness not just in Jerusalem, but in Judea and Samaria, and to the ends of the earth.

Luke's message about what is involved in the learning curve for healing therefore needs to be seen from cover to cover. If we will stay with the tough experience of the troughs, the undertow, and the gap between where we are and where we want to be, God will take us forward on the journey of learning. What makes the difference between those who keep on 'Route D', staying with all that is involved, and those who plateau prematurely, is the extent of our hunger to see God work through us. It depends on what we are truly yearning for in our hearts. A life which maintains our comfort, or one which prioritizes learning more of how to become available to

God, that healing might be ministered through us to a hurting and lost world. Unfortunately such learning cannot be painless, because it has to touch the roots of our self-centredness if we are to become increasingly God-centred. However, in a mature model of healing, to fail need not mean we are failures. Through the pain can come the gain.

15

Why Pray 'Come Holy Spirit'?

I f the essence of a mature healing ministry is 'learning by doing', in which those who minister healing must be willing to put at stake who and what they are, this raises a further question. What are we to make of the response of the Holy Spirit to the prayer inviting Him 'to come'? John Wimber has shown that there is a way of inviting the Holy Spirit in the ministry of healing which can result in some amazing things happening. The Spirit's response can be staggering, both metaphorically and literally, and we may need to do very little other than to bless what He is doing. Is this however the definitive understanding of co-operation with the Holy Spirit in the healing ministry? Or is the Holy Spirit inviting us to consider something beyond the immediacy of the extraordinary phenomena He sometimes releases in people?

The invitation to the Holy Spirit 'to come' is in fact an ancient prayer. In medieval times, when the hymn *'Veni Creator Spiritus'* (literally, Come, Holy Spirit) was written, it was surrounded in mystical tradition. It was about the intuitive experience of the spiritual. Yet it goes back much further than this. Its roots are in the eucharistic prayer of the Eastern Church for the Holy Spirit to change the bread and wine into the literal body and blood of Christ. This was known as 'epiclesis'. By contrast, the present understanding of the invitation to the Holy Spirit 'to come' seems somewhat cosmetic. It overlooks the awesomeness of the One we are inviting. The phrase seems to have become little more than a

form of words, hopefully through which to expedite healing. A more mature understanding of why we should
pray 'Come Holy Spirit' would seem to be increasingly
necessary.

Let us begin by thinking about how the Holy Spirit
must feel to be inundated with so many pressing invitations 'to come'! Not every one will be exactly the type
He might want to say yes to. Even more importantly, how
does He feel about the invitations He has made to His
people to come closer to Him that have gone unheeded?

The decision to accept an invitation depends at least
in part on why we think our presence is desired. Is it
for who we are to the people who have invited us, or
for what they think we can do for them? This distinction
came home to me one night when as a treat our girls slept
outside in the tent. They were making the most of every
moment of it. In her prayers my elder daughter prayed
a world-tour expression of thankfulness. Eventually she
rounded off with extended gratitude for her sister, next
her mother, and finally she came to me. Then followed a
long pause. I waited with bated breath to hear what she
would thank God for in me. At last she began. 'Thank you
God for Daddy . . . because he can mend things, Amen.'

I would have felt hurt, except for something which had
happened a few weeks earlier. It was when Françoise and
the girls were flying home from Los Angeles, leaving me
to continue my sabbatical. Suddenly, in the middle of the
bustle of the airport she stopped to say to me 'Daddy, I
love you'. Fathers carry such memories in their hearts
for a long while. I knew her appreciation of my ability to
put toys back together was set in the greater context of
her love for me. If there was a toy I couldn't fix, I knew
she would still love me and want to be with me.

Not all our relationships are like that. For example,
if when the man we have asked to come to repair the
washing machine has finished, we are not so keen on
his continued presence. He is only wanted for what he
can mend. Though we may do it unwittingly, if we just

invite the Holy Spirit for the healing He can bring, we can put our relationship with Him into the 'repair man' category. His heart is for a vastly greater relationship with us, which is as much about us coming to Him, as it is about Him coming to us. Indeed, it is only as we choose to move closer to Him that He can draw us forwards on the journey of learning we have been considering.

The most succinct description of the relationship the Holy Spirit wants to have with us is the well-known, but not so well-understood, blessing 'the grace of the Lord Jesus Christ, and the love of God, and the fellowship of the Holy Spirit be with you all' (2 Corinthians 13:14). Charismatic Christians readily interpret the fellowship of the Holy Spirit through the baptism and gifts of the Holy Spirit. Yet the 'fellowship with the Holy Spirit' is about a far more reciprocal relationship than this.

Fellowship in this context means communion, in the sense of intimate presence, sharing together as hearts are poured out to each other. It means friendship in which there are no secrets. This is what the Holy Spirit longs to have with us. Indeed it would seem to be the key to being led of Him on the learning journey He would have us travel. When eagerness for charismatic gifts is the priority, such understanding of fellowship with the Spirit can be quite overlooked. Enthusiasm for the gifts of the Spirit does not necessarily mean a quality relationship with the Giver.

In such enthusiasm we may be unaware of our effect on the One whose desire is as much to be with us, as to do through us. His nature is such that how we relate to Him causes Him either to give or to grieve. To want Him only for what we can get out of Him, through healing or the experience of other gifts, can cause Him grief. We are strongly warned against this (Ephesians 4:30). Such grief means anguish of body and mind, which can cause a pulling back, a quenching or a putting out of the fire of the relationship He wants to have with us. As He withdraws from close proximity to us, the opportunity to detect His sensitive leading of us can be greatly reduced.

His response, however, may go much further, as the people of Israel discovered when they rebelled and grieved Him. He literally turned and became their enemy, and it was He who fought against them (Isaiah 63:10). In the New Testament, serious warning is given to any who insult the 'Spirit of grace' (Hebrews 10:29). David recognized that sin could cause the Holy Spirit to withdraw. It was something he saw to be so serious, he pleaded with God it should not be allowed to happen (Psalm 51:11). To continue to be led of the Spirit on the journey of learning may therefore require repentance over where we have grieved Him. We may need to humble ourselves afresh to enter into the more mature communion He desires to have with us.

The gift of the Spirit's fellowship in healing

Even Jesus' earthly ministry of healing depended on fellowship with the Spirit. Though the Son of God, the works He did were those of the supremely Spirit-filled man. His commission to the disciples to carry forward His ministry therefore centred on their receiving the gift of fellowship with the Spirit, even before the gift of healing.

It was this the resurrected Jesus ministered to the fearful disciples when He appeared to them in the locked room. Twice He said 'Peace be with you', the second time continuing 'As the Father has sent me, I am sending you'. He then breathed on them and said 'Receive the Holy Spirit' (John 20:19–22). Without it they had good reason to be fearful about continuing Jesus' ministry. Later on however they were to discover how they had been gifted to do the works of Jesus primarily through fellowship with the Spirit, rather than through charismatic ability. We equally need fellowship with the Spirit, even more than charismatic giftedness, if we are also to do the works of Jesus, and it is this that should be the true focus of the prayer which says 'Come, Holy Spirit'.

In Romans 8:1–27 there is a list of eight specific areas the Holy Spirit wants to come and fellowship with us in. The extent to which our doors are open in each of these areas to saying 'Come Holy Spirit' greatly affects what we can expect to happen when we pray it for others. The eight areas are:

1) Choosing to live in freedom from the past

'The law of the Spirit of life set me free from the law of sin and death' (v2). It remains with us though as to how much of that freedom we actually live in. A woman once came to me with, she said, an important word from the Lord. Anticipating some extensive discourse, I was somewhat thrown when she simply said 'God says you're no angel' and walked away! Of itself, this was no new revelation. Until I realized what the word was actually about. Angels do not have free will as I do. It was up to me to choose whether I would live under the influence of my past, or in the light of my future. God has brought me out from under condemnation, and the full evidence of that will one day be seen. How much it is seen in me now depends on the choices I make. All healing involves a choice to respond to what has been offered the opportunity to be set free. We can only minister that choosing of freedom in so far as we know it to be a living reality within ourselves.

2) Choosing to set our minds on the things of the Spirit

'The mind controlled by the Spirit is life and peace' (v6). Despite the completeness of our salvation, the question remains of what our minds are really set on. An acid test is how we react to loss. I heard a Christian talking of how his reactions to losing something minor were exposed by his friend's reaction to losing his business, his house, and

many possessions. 'The thing about Dan', he said 'is that
he hasn't changed through all that has happened.' Dan
was well known for his heart being set on the things of
the Spirit. He had lost much which was precious, but
not what was most precious. He still had life and peace
in the Spirit. Living amidst Western society, we cannot
avoid interacting with its materialism, but it is up to us
whether or not we become entangled with it. We need
the conviction of the Spirit to reveal what our hearts are
actually set upon. He will not force this on us. It is our
choice whether or not we allow Him to control what goes
on in our mind.

3) Choosing the vitality of the Spirit
'He . . . will also give life to your mortal bodies through
his Spirit' (v11). The Spirit who comes to fellowship
with us is the One who raised Jesus from the dead.
Even before the resurrection, God's power was known
to 'give strength to the weary and increases the power
of the weak' (Isaiah 40:29). What we now also have
is the presence of the resurrected One in our lives.
We therefore have enormous potential for living in the
vitality of the Spirit. This is not the same as the Faith
Movement's declaration that we have the right to walk
in divine health. What it does mean is that we may have
a vitality of the Spirit that strengthens and empowers
even those who are weak and weary.

When I was walking one day with Françoise along a
country lane, she turned abruptly to go back to a car we
had just walked past. She had seen an older lady sitting
in it, who, it transpired, was a missionary she had known
some years earlier. What had struck Françoise however
was not the recognition of her face, but the light she had
seen in it. Only later did she realize who the lady was.
It was the vitality of the Spirit she had seen, perhaps
a glimpse of the same radiance that was on Moses'
face as he came down the mountain from being with
the Lord (Exodus 34:29–35). Such renewal of the inner

being that shines through the flesh demonstrates that how our flesh feels, even be it unwell or aging, is not the final determinant of how we are.

4) Choosing the way of holiness

'If by the Spirit you will put to death the misdeeds of the body, you will live' (v13). Whereas holiness is a fundamental attribute of God, for us it is a choice. It means putting the axe to the root of the lie which C.S. Lewis pinpointed when he wrote 'But mere time does nothing either to the facts or the guilt of a sin. The guilt is washed out not by time but by repentance and the blood of Christ.[1] Something within us suggests that the effect of sin in our lives diminishes in proportion to how long ago it was. The Spirit's desire is to show the need for all that has gone on in our lives to be washed. Though the ministry of healing does not depend on personal holiness, lack of it can nonetheless block the flow of the grace.

Talking with a dying lady, I asked how she felt about what lay ahead. She responded wistfully, 'We can but hope'. It was clear she had no confidence in the work of grace in her life. I prayed for something that would give a breakthrough that a lifetime in church never had. The Lord gave a picture of her washing up, as she had done after many meals shared with others. I asked if anyone had ever asked whether her plates were clean enough to eat off in view of all the visitors who had used them before. Almost indignantly she explained that when she washed a plate, no matter how dirty it had become, it would be spotless by the time she had finished with it. It was a wonderful opening to explain the cleansing Christ's blood gives to all who will choose to wash in it.

5) Choosing to receive the spirit of sonship

'Those who are led by the Spirit of God are sons of God' (v14). To minister healing effectively requires confidence in one's relationship with God as Father. As children

trust their earthly fathers to act in their best interests
even if they don't understand what is going on, so we
need to trust God. Yet whilst it is true in principle that
we are God's children, what that means in practice can
take time to work through. There may be many reasons
why we find it difficult to receive the fullness of the spirit
of sonship which cries '*Abba*, Father' (v15). However,
the Spirit's desire is to testify with our spirit that we
are God's children (v16). The extent to which we know
that depends however on our openness (to use Tom
Smail's quote of H.H. Farmer) to God being 'absolute
demand and ultimate succour'.[2] Our willingness to go
into circumstances we wouldn't go near if it weren't for
God's leading is a big factor in discovering that God is
the Father who does not fail His children.

6) Choosing to live under the guarantee of what is to come

'We ... who have the firstfruits of the Spirit' (v23).
Firstfruits are a picture of what is to come, the significance of which originated in the giving of the Law at Sinai.
In it was the command to celebrate the Feast of Harvest
on arrival in the Promised Land, using the firstfruits of
the harvest. They were a token which stood between what
had been promised having been fulfilled, and the fullness
of the promise which was yet to be seen, but which was
now certain. Even in our society, firstfruits still have a
special value, such as the worth of the very first Mini
ever produced at Longbridge even though millions of
remarkably similar cars have since been produced.

However, in the New Testament, firstfruits take on
a new and even greater significance. They move from
what was given back by man to God, to what God gives
to man as the token of the promise He will fulfil. So
Jesus is described as the firstfruits of the resurrection
from the dead (1 Corinthians 15:23). We do not yet see
all in Christ being made alive, but the fact that He is
risen means that totality of resurrection will happen.

For us to be described as having the firstfruits of the Spirit therefore points to the inexorable fulfilment of what is promised in us. We may feel in the healing ministry that we are a very long way off a harvest of any substance. The accuser may point to the diminutive size of the harvest we have to show for it. Yet even if we have ministered only a tiny amount of healing, we have firstfruits which he has no answer to. We need to choose to live in the light of the guarantee they represent.

7) Choosing the way of weakness

'The Spirit helps us in our weakness' (v26). Natural tendency is to play to our strengths rather than our weaknesses, yet God has chosen the way of foolishness and weakness through which to manifest His power. To be used of God, this is where we need to be. Scripture includes many instances of how God has either led His people into the place of weakness before using them, or chosen to use them because of their weakness. Moses needed Aaron to speak publicly for him. Joshua had to take Jericho by walking round it in circles for seven days. Gideon had to have his army reduced from 32,000 down to 300 before the Midianites could be defeated. Jeremiah was anxious about speaking because he was only a youth. Hosea had to marry a harlot, that God might speak through his marriage. Even Paul had to come to the Corinthians in weakness and fear, and with much trembling. Most telling of all is the description of Christ as the Suffering Servant, who would 'bring justice to the nations. He will not shout or cry out ... A bruised reed he will not break, and a smouldering wick he will not snuff out' (Isaiah 42:1–3).

The paradox is that the most powerful place to minister healing can be the place of weakness. It is also the best place to be for meeting those whose need of healing has left them in weakness.

8) Choosing the prayer of the Spirit

'We do not know what we ought to pray for, but the Spirit himself intercedes for us with groans that words cannot express' (v26). All we can do in the ministry of healing is to intercede for others. Yet the fact is that the intercession which results in healing does not originate in us. Instead it begins at the Father's right hand as Jesus intercedes for the continued outworking of His saving purposes on earth (Hebrews 7:25). It is the Spirit who links the intercession around the throne of God to the intercession for healing which takes place through us. Without the Spirit's part there would be no connection between the supernatural power of God to heal, and the natural things of this world which so desperately need healing. It is however an immensely costly ministry for the Spirit which involves Him in the expression of yearnings too deep for utterance. We cannot expect to truly participate in it without willingness to experience something of the Spirit's groaning.

A mature understanding of why we should pray for the Holy Spirit 'to come' is therefore not as a formula to precipitate effortless healing in others. It is an invitation for the Spirit to come into what these eight areas represent in our lives. In doing so to transform what is found within. The purpose of this is that we might be more able to come and fellowship with Him however and wherever He may want that to be. 'Come, Holy Spirit', notwithstanding its dramatic place in 'power healing', is therefore more about 'power fellowship'. The former may well have an effortless feel to it, but the latter is quite the opposite. It is about repentance, learning and change. Yet if we will travel such journey with Him, along the way the Holy Spirit will make us more whole. As He does this, so we will become better equipped for a mature ministry of healing to others.

The ultimate aim of the Spirit is not though for any one-off need of healing to be met. It is that with an absolutely united voice the church, who is the bride, will be able to join with Him to say 'Come!' The invitation then will be to whoever is thirsty, that he might come and take the free gift of the water of life (Revelation 22:17). It is the crowning fellowship of complete oneness of heart that the Holy Spirit wants us to come into with Him. Through this will be ushered in an even greater coming, which will precipitate the final healing of all things.

16

Can We See What God Wants To Heal?

Sitting in the garden, I began to sip a can of lager. Suddenly an acute pain passed through my lungs from the top to the bottom. It was a shocking experience that left me wondering whatever was happening. Yet by the evening I was feeling noticeably better than I had for a long while. What had not happened during all the prayer I had received for the sarcoidosis in my lungs had now begun to happen quite unpredictably. During the months that followed, a progressive healing continued to take place. I must confess I was drinking the lager that claims to refresh you in the places no other lager does! I suspected though that there was another explanation.

Throughout my reflections on the healing ministry, I had sought to get into what God might be saying through the tough questions there are about it. My premise was that they were His invitations to discover what a more mature ministry of healing might look like. I had long since decided that though miracles of healing do still happen, these were not to be the goal we are to aspire to as a normative model of healing. Healing can come as a miracle, in terms of God's sudden intervention to bring total restoration of a specific health problem. Indeed there will be occasions such as in a crisis, or when we are seeking an in-break for evangelism, that we not only may, but indeed should, pray for miracles of healing. However, God's desire is not first and foremost to impose His glory through spectacular interventions. It is for glory to be given by mankind voluntarily choosing to worship Him, even if things aren't exactly as he would want.

My conclusion had been that though we may expect acceleration of the normal healing processes as we pray, God has a bigger vision of what healing is about which He will accomplish on His own timescale. His concern is more to renew the damaged but often hidden parts of our being rather than simply to restore our capacity to do. We may not be able to explain why things happen to us as they do, but God still wants to minister wholeness to us through all the events of life, even those we perceive as bad. A response of faith is needed for this, not as a formula, but as trust is humbly expressed in God's power to redeem. Within the sovereignty of God, not all that redemption will be seen in this world. However, there is an eternal perspective, that of the 'not yet' in which the fullness of healing will be seen.

I had considered the distinction between healing which needed deliverance ministry, that which was psychological, requiring the taking of personal responsibility, and that which is psychosomatic, in which the complex interplay of body, soul and spirit has to be taken account of. My thinking had gone beyond the healing of the individual to the greater importance of healing of society, and the part of individuals in it. I had reflected on how God harnesses our mistakes, rather than just baling us out of them. His purpose is to enable us to learn how we may be used for the coming of the Holy Spirit that others may be healed.

Though I didn't think of it as a miracle I experienced in the garden, it still contributed significantly to my subsequent recovery. Curiously though, through my reflections on what might constitute a more mature model of healing, I had come to terms with the absence of any sudden intervention of God in my recovery. Was what I felt just one of those things, or had I after all had some form of intervention from God? If so, much as I appreciated it, I found it hard to see what God was

doing touching me in this way. It led me on to consider
what Jesus meant by His 'only doing what he sees the
Father doing' (John 5:19) and our ability, or otherwise,
to see what He is doing. Despite all the complexities of
the healing ministry, should our goal be to see that easily
what God is doing?

I had to admit that my reflections on the ministry of
healing had been far from easy. I could see how the
Father had clearly led me to do some reflecting on it,
but it was rather less obvious from then on. Everything
was hard-won through grappling with tough questions.
Was it that Jesus just looked and saw exactly what
the Father was doing with some form of spiritual X-ray
vision? Or did Jesus also only see what the Father was
doing by grappling with tough questions that He had no
easy answers to? What do we learn from the example
of Jesus about seeing what God wants to do in healing,
especially as we consider what the way ahead for a more
mature ministry of healing might be?

The question of the extent to which the fullness of
humanity was expressed in Christ, as well as the fullness
of divinity, is one of the classic theological debates. Many
complex treatises have been written on it. However, one
thing is made crystal clear by the Gospel writers. Jesus
died with an unanswered question on His lips. 'About the
ninth hour Jesus cried out in a loud voice, *"Eloi, Eloi, lama
sabachthani?"* – which means, "My God, My God, why have
you forsaken me?"' (Matthew 27:46, Mark 15:33).

Notwithstanding Jesus' absolute certainty about the
need to go the way of the cross, through which the healing
of all things was to come, it still involved having to go
through the toughest question that has ever been asked
in all eternity. As Jesus quoted the opening words of
Psalm 22:1 to utter His cry of dereliction, He questioned
the separation of Father and Son. In that moment there
was no answer. Yet because He chose to press forwards
in the face of not seeing an answer, healing was won for
all creation. Certainly there was absolute uniqueness in

the person of Jesus Christ, which inevitably enabled Him to minister healing in ways we never will be able to. We cannot stand where He stood. Yet, as He became sin on the cross for our sake, He stood where we stand. He entered into the place of question in healing where there are no easy answers to be seen.

We may wonder whether asking so many questions about healing impairs or improves performance. We may wonder whether it isn't better just to stick with our simple precepts and avoid the complexities. However, the words of Jesus from the cross suggest that the fullness of God's healing purposes are only to be found as we press forward into the tough questions we are faced with, however unanswerable they may seem to be.

Having sought to consider some of the tough questions which arise out of our practice of healing, two other questions remain which we therefore also need to press into the face of, however hard it is to see what the answers might be. Firstly, as we look at where our society presently stands, what might God be saying about how our expression of healing can be made more relevant? Secondly, how in practical terms should the church seek to press forwards with the healing ministry from where it is now. We turn to these questions in this and the final chapter.

Seeing where society needs healing

It is with a plaintive voice that society cries out for healing. Yet we need to see where it needs healing if we are to reach out to it with relevance. This is not something God will show us just like that. We need to grapple with the tough questions about the signs of the times if we are to see what God is wanting to heal.

Whereas in the sixties there was deep uncertainty about the atom bomb, and whether we would all be blown up through some international catastrophe, it is a very different sort of unease we now live with. It now

concerns the widespread feeling that the material gains
of the eighties have simply not satisfied peoples' deepest
needs. There is a justified discontent in those who have
found that economic returns are no compensation for
social and moral ills, that they are just not worth the
price that was paid for them. As Bishop Michael Marshall
has suggested, the epitaph of our civilisation might well
read 'Everything to live with and nothing to live for'. The
pursuit of materialism has meant that instead of using
things and loving people, society has fallen for loving
things and using people.

Worse still, the fragile worth of the diminishing returns
of capitalism has been exposed by the economic downturn
of the nineties. The vulnerability of such consumerist
gains as there have been has been harshly exposed.
Paradoxically, this has resulted in both East and West
being faced from opposite directions with the identical
lesson. It is about the erroneous doctrine of economic
determinism, which preaches the shaping of history not
by spiritual, but by economic forces.

Many factors contributed to the fall of communism, not
least of which was its fundamental error that man is good
and utopia can be built by human endeavour. However,
the temptation for the West has been to assume that in
the winning of the cold war there has been the vindication
of the free market over and against communism. Communism ultimately collapsed because of what was going
on in the hearts of the peoples of the Eastern bloc. No
amount of tyrannical repression could prevent it, and no
amount of satellite technology which can count the bolts
on a tank could observe it. It was the inward hunger for
spiritual truth and life which precipitated its demise.

In the West, the deficiency of capitalism to provide
the answers which are most wanted is now also being
revealed. Though it is a totally different form of economic
determinism, capitalism is being seen as having no more
ability of itself to meet the spiritual needs of mankind
than communism had. What is happening in the West is

like a counterpoint to what has happened in the East. It
is therefore not surprising that even the secular prophets
are speaking of the imminence of some form of religious
revival, in both the West and the East. However, the West
faces a particular spiritual danger. It has had a far longer
history of freedom of thought and opportunity to try new
things. Given the depth of desire for spiritual reality and
the degree of the spiritual vacuum, it is no surprise that
the prophecies of a religious revival in the West are not
necessarily of a Christian one.

One example of the competition now confronting the
Western church is the rapid advance of the New Age
movement. So far the greatest impact has been in
America, but what grips the American mind soon grips
the British mind. Already it is estimated that of the 2,000
religious books published each year in Britain, around one
quarter will be on a New Age topic. New Age evangelist,
Shirley MacLaine is quoted as saying

> Millions of people all over the world are so interested
> in this stuff that they support an entire industry of
> books, teachings, schools, individuals and literature
> of all kinds devoted to the metaphysical dimensions
> of life. I wouldn't call it occult. I would call it an
> interest in the spiritual dimension of life.[1]

Interest in New Age is not restricted to those on the
fringes of society. It is being increasingly embraced by
large numbers of intelligent people across the spectrum
of life. New Age theories and practices are insidiously
finding their way into ecology, medicine, business, educa-
tion and so on. The reason is that it offers a smorgasbord
of ways to fill the spiritual chasm in life which the church
has not filled. Much of it appears to fit the needs and aspi-
rations of Western society very well. Amongst the things
on offer is the prospect of self-development potential and
personal fulfilment, such as the notion of 'that which you

can conceive and believe in, you can achieve.' It promotes
the idea of transformation to a new level of consciousness.
It professes concern for conservation, world peace and
harmony. In the awareness of the mess the world is in,
and the need for change, it can all seem rather enticing.

The New Age movement is the consequence of man's
dissatisfaction with spiritual vacuum. It has been said
that 'Secular man killed a God in whom he could not
believe, but whose absence he could not bear.' What
has been come up with to fill the void is an extraordinary concoction of cults, occult, theosophy, astrol-
ogy, ancient gnosticism and Eastern mysticism. To try
to describe it has been likened to trying to wrestle
with jelly.

However, underneath its power to give superficial
release are a swarm of octopus-like tentacles out to trap
and destroy those who would venture close enough to be
caught. Despite its use of expressions and symbols which
seem almost Christian, there is the fundamental denial
of a personal God, that Jesus is the Christ, indeed of the
realities of sin, evil and death. It is centred on 'monism',
which teaches that man, God and everything are one,
and pantheism, which teaches that God is an impersonal
force that permeates everything. Effectively it is teaching
that 'all is one' and 'all is God'. The corollary of this
is that humanity is God and man is therefore his own
saviour.

Notwithstanding the counterfeit nature of the New
Age, its emphasis on both the spiritual and the need for
reality, meaning and purpose, can make it deceptively
attractive. In the present climate of hunger for spiritual
truth it is not surprising that it is winning an increasing
following. It looks sufficiently like the real thing to be
plausible to a wide cross-section of people. It is capable
of changing people's worldview. If the prophecies of religious revival are correct, its subtle power to influence, on
top of that of all the other religious influences, must not
be underestimated.

The challenge to the church

The challenge to the church in the face of this is to do far more than simply plan a defence against getting walked over. The challenge is to see how God wants to bring healing to society where it truly hurts, in a way beyond that which New Age or any other religious system is capable of. Whether we do will depend on the extent to which the church is willing to grapple sufficiently with the relevant questions, however hard it might be to see where the answers lie. Once, sitting in a restaurant furnished with World War II memorabilia, I found myself being stared at by a picture of Winston Churchill. He was pointing in my direction saying 'Deserve Victory!' Which way the spiritual battle will swing in the spiritual vortex of the coming years will depend very much on what we as a church deserve.

The risk of the present enthusiasm for the Decade of Evangelism is that it can rest too much on what the church thinks itself capable of and not enough on seeing what God wants to touch. The story of what happened to those who went up to take Ai (Joshua 7:1–6) is a salutary warning. Following the dramatic capture of Jericho, spies were sent to survey Ai. Their assessment was that not all the people were needed to go up to take the city: two to three thousand should suffice. Just that number went, but they were routed, so that the hearts of the people of Israel melted and became like water. The reason for their defeat was that there had been sin within them which had not been repented of. However much God wants to advance His purposes through His people as they seek to press forwards, it still depends on rightness of relationship with Him.

It is therefore potentially hazardous for the church to press into the eye of the developing spiritual battle without first seeing where God may be wanting it to repent. Otherwise, the danger is, that around the year 2000, amidst the post-millennial anti-climax that will inevitably follow all the hype, the same may possibly happen to the church that happened to the 2,000 or so who went up to Ai. The church will have played all its big cards in the preceding ten years. Whatever the victories of the decade, should the church find itself routed at that point there could be long-term loss for it. The heart of the people might indeed melt when whatever is by then under the umbrella of the New Age movement gets its big opportunity.

For the church to repent of the sin that has been in its camp, that will have to include seeing the uncomfortable truth of the maxim that the 'cults are the unpaid bills of the Christian church'. We need to hear as one body, and as individuals, what God is saying about our responsibility for the post-Christian spiritual vacuum we have allowed to go unfilled. Particularly for how it has left hunger for spiritual truth to go unsatisfied and provided the opportunity for New Age thinking to take root. Without seeing how God may first want to heal the church through such repentance, we may not have much basis to stand on. We must not delude ourselves: it was the same God who enabled victory at Jericho that allowed defeat at Ai to follow so swiftly.

It is vital that the church does not sidestep these issues. Modern society has enormous need of a church that has faced for itself the questions about healing from the individual to the corporate, as well as for the lost world it seeks to minister to. The church's ability to see what God wants to heal in society can be no greater than its own willingness to see what needs healing within it. Tough questions need to be properly faced, not just about what constitutes a more mature ministry of healing, but of the church's competence to minister such healing. If they are genuinely grappled with, then the God who can suddenly touch and restore individuals when they least expect it, can similarly touch the church and restore its ability to see what He truly wants to heal.

17

How Do We Go Forward From Here?

For the church to move forward in the ministry of healing it will require more than just good intention. The church is well-versed in the art of looking as if it's about to do something without ever actually doing it.

When, as a theological student in Durham, I daily chugged on my moped past the magnificent monument of a former Lord Lieutenant on rampant horseback that dominates the city's Market Place, I often thought of how Cardinal Newman described the church as being

> like an equestrian statue: the front legs are lifted up ready to leap forward, every muscle of the back legs is standing out throbbing with life. As you look at the statue, you expect it to spring forward at any moment. Unfortunately, when you come back twenty years later, it has not moved a fraction of an inch. Yet look at the early church twenty years after the outpouring of the Spirit . . . they had moved forwards by astonishing leaps and bounds. There was one simple reason . . . the power of the Holy Spirit was with them.

However much the gradient slowed my moped, I consoled myself that at least I was progressing up the slope better than the man on his horse. The tough question for the church is what will enable it to progress in the healing ministry from here.

The possibilities for the healing ministry to play a

substantial part in the proclamation of the gospel, not only
through the Decade of Evangelism, but through into the
next millennium are very real. To quote George Bernard
Shaw: 'you see things as they are and ask "Why?" But I
dream things that never were and ask, "Why not?" With
the eye of faith we can see the opportunity that lies ahead.
There is a hunger in society for spiritual truth, and the
fields are more and more ready for harvest. We have a
new order of ecumenical opportunity, and in at least some
sections of the church there is a heart of real expectancy. A
powerful ministry of healing that is manifestly seen to work
in touching both society and individuals could do much to
endorse the proclamation of the gospel.

Yet with the eye of history we can see the vulnerability
of it all. It will require special action if the healing
ministry is to mature and to capture the opportunity.
Otherwise it will get stuck in the position of promising
massive movement, but never actually going anywhere.
We have been greatly privileged to have John Wimber
and others move us thus far. It is wrong however to go
on looking to God to send us more such leaders to exercise
initiative on our behalf.

It is for us to own our responsibility for pressing
forwards in the healing ministry. Paul's words describe
the attitude we need:

> I press on to take hold of that for which Christ Jesus
> took hold of me. Brothers, I do not consider myself
> yet to have taken hold of it. But one thing I do:
> Forgetting what is behind and straining towards
> what is ahead, I press on towards the goal to win
> the prize for which God has called me heavenwards
> in Christ Jesus. All of us who are mature should take
> such a view of things.
>
>   (Philippians 3:12–15)

It is not just a more mature model of healing that
is needed, but a more mature approach to it, which

recognizes that it is now up to us to take the necessary initiatives.

The 'forgetting what is behind' should not be taken to permit any disrespect for the good foundations we have been given for the healing ministry. Indeed Paul goes on to say 'Only let us live up to what we have already attained' (v16). We need to value what we have been given. It is like petrol which in the tank of a car can fuel it for a tremendous distance, or can equally vaporise at a remarkable rate if it is spilt. To capitalize on what we have been given will involve us recognizing what a mature attitude to the healing ministry should now be about. The priority is for the development of an indigenous healing ministry rather than one which still depends on the importing of big-name speakers. Otherwise there will always be an implicit understanding of it as something brought into us from outside, rather than something we are meant to be exporting to the world outside.

It is from this perspective that seed-thoughts for three lines of action are suggested. They are offered as ways to enable us to grasp the opportunity within our personal lives, our local churches, our city-wide relationships with other Christians and our church at national level.

1) Taking prophetic initiatives in healing

When we look at all the tough questions there are about the healing ministry, we may feel something of what the prophet Ezekiel felt when he found himself amidst the valley of dry bones. As he was led to and fro amongst them he observed that the bones looked very dry. The Lord asked him 'Son of man, can these bones live?' We may well want to reply with him 'O Sovereign Lord, you alone know' (Ezekiel 37:3).

God's word to Ezekiel was unequivocal.

'Prophesy to these bones and say to them, "Dry bones, hear the word of the Lord! This is what the

Sovereign Lord says to these bones: I will make
breath enter you, and you will come to life. I will
attach tendons to you and make flesh come upon
you and cover you with skin; I will put breath in
you, and you will come to life. Then you will know
that I am the Lord."'

(Ezekiel 37:4–6)

So God's word is to us. We are to be a prophetic people,
whose vision is ultimately for the healing of all that seems
dead. It is a vision which needs to begin within each of us,
but then to extend to the full sweep of the church from the
local to the national.

Ezekiel was obedient and prophesied as he was commanded. First there was a noise, then a rattling sound
as the bones came together, bone to bone. Tendons and
flesh appeared on them and skin covered them, but there
was no breath in them. Structure had been reformed, the
potential for life was there, but without the breath, there
was no life. The vision for healing, both in and through the
church is the same. The renewal of structures by itself is
not enough. The breath of the Spirit is essential. Ezekiel
was commanded to prophesy again that breath might
enter and life might return. Once more he obeyed, life
came back into the bodies, and they stood up on their
feet – a vast army.

Then God said to Ezekiel

'Son of man, these bones are the whole house of
Israel. They say "Our bones are dried up and our
hope is gone; we are cut off." Therefore prophesy
and say to them: "This is what the Sovereign Lord
says: O my people, I am going to open your graves
and bring you up from them; I will bring you back
to the land of Israel . . . Then you will know that I
the Lord have spoken, and I have done it, declares
the Lord."'

(vv 11–14)

It was only as Ezekiel kept prophesying in obedience to what God was saying that the full restoration of God's people took place. The vision was that only as he acted a stage at a time did God move to accomplish His purposes.

A massive healing involving national restoration was envisioned as a result of Ezekiel's prophetic action when he obeyed God's leading. However symbolic this passage is, its message is clear. Whether it is in our personal lives and spheres of influence, in our local church situations, or in our broader church relationships, God's capacity to heal is beyond our comprehension. However, He exercises His power to break in to what seems dead only insofar as prophetic initiative is obediently taken. We therefore need to hear from Him what those prophetic initiatives are that He is calling us to.

2) Organizing properly for healing

The fact that God's healing power may come unpredictably can divert us from the need to organize as we press on towards the goal. Organization can be bureaucratic and unspiritual, and may serve only to dampen God's power as it breaks in. It may seem like the last requirement for the healing power of God to be manifest amongst us. The danger however is to think that the solution is in the other extreme. Advances in the ministry of healing will not happen spontaneously. We need to note how Jesus in fact modelled an organized approach to introducing healing into the world.

In *Vision Building* Peter Brierley suggests that church organization should have a back-cloth that relates its overall purpose down to its specific actions (see figure 1).[1] In his terminology, the statement of 'purpose' defines what we are about. How we do that is our 'mission', and what in practice this will mean is our 'vision'. Out of this emerges the 'thrusts' which are our key lines of action, and our 'goals' which are the range of targets we will set ourselves for achieving them. 'Priorities'

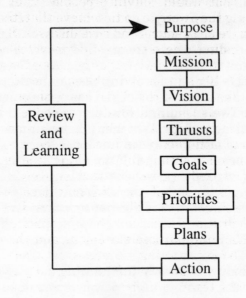

Figure 1.

are the key things needed for achieving our targets, and 'plans' specify the things we will do as a result of all this. 'Action' and 'review and learning' speak for themselves! However businesslike and cumbersome this might appear it can be seen in the way Jesus sent out the Twelve on the first healing expedition.

The *purpose* Jesus gave them was to exercise His power and authority (Luke 9:1). This was what they were to be about in the future: it was to be the foundation for the extension of His ministry on earth. How it was to happen, their *mission*, was (v2) to go out preaching the kingdom of God and healing the sick. What in practice this was to mean, their *vision*, was (v3) of an empty-handed journey through the villages during which they should be looking to see God's hand at work. Their key line of action, their *thrust* was (vv4,5) to get into homes. Their *goal*, or their target, having got into a home was to do signs and wonders that would convince people about Jesus. The main thing they were to do to achieve that, their *priority*, was to drive out demons and cure diseases. So they made *plans*, deciding where to go, and the *action* resulted as they went. *Review and learning* happened when they returned (v10) and shared all that had happened. We need to take stock of the organized basis on which Jesus sent the Twelve out and what happened as a result. The Twelve clearly understood what they were about, and the in-break of God took place in consequence.

Perhaps one reason why we do not see more of such in-break of God's power, is because we do not have a sharper perception of the different elements of what we are seeking to do. What is so often done in church life, and in the healing ministry in particular, is to go for the headline purpose statement and then jump into action. The intervening elements get over-looked. The consequence is that what we are actually about doesn't get thought through properly. As a result less happens than otherwise might, and the opportunity for review and learning is greatly diminished.

The message of the first healing mission is not just about the way God can break in when His people move out seeking to express His healing power. It is also about the part that appropriate organization needs to play in it. It has been said that 'no one plans to fail, but many fail to plan'. A vital part of pressing towards the goal in the healing ministry is the fullest thinking through of what we're doing and why.

3) Processing our understanding of healing

Prophetic initiative and proper organization are vital to the healing ministry, but are still not enough. The third component we need is the continued processing of what we learn about healing as we go along. This means openness to new agendas in healing that the on-going tough questions will raise. We are to keep pressing forwards on the learning curve of healing, through all the ups and downs. Otherwise we will at best plateau, but more probably go into a progressive decline. Paul's overriding concern was that he was not running in vain (Galatians 2:2, Philippians 2:16). If, with all the self-evident consequences of what he did, he felt such urgent need to review what was resulting from his ministry, how much more must we.

For Paul, there were two very different things he sought to review. There was the knowing of the power of the resurrection, and the sharing of the fellowship of Christ's sufferings (Philippians 3:10). The emphasis in healing has so far been more on the former than the latter. The re-discovery of power healing, especially as it relates to evangelism has been very good. So has been the rediscovery of pastoral healing, that the saints might not be so held back in their living for the Lord. Perhaps that which most needs to be learnt about now is 'paschal' healing, which reflects what emerges from fellowship with the suffering of the slain Lamb.

It may prove to be the way through into greater maturity in the healing ministry, which could enable the emerging issues of our day to be tackled. If society does move increasingly towards seeking spiritual answers to its problems, one thing to be countered with great effectiveness will be the New Age doctrine of man as his own saviour. Paschal healing puts the emphasis in the opposite direction entirely. It will require learning how, through our lives, to echo the loudness of the voice of the many angels numbering ten thousand times ten thousand who John saw singing 'Worthy is the Lamb, who was slain, to receive power and wealth and wisdom and strength and honour and glory and praise!' (Revelation 5:12). What they saw in the Lamb who was slain were the very things that people have looked for in this world, yet failed to find. We need by the distinctiveness of our lives to point to where they may be found for all eternity. It means learning more about knowing Christ, not only in the power of His resurrection, but also in the fellowship of His sufferings, becoming like Him in His death.

This may appear somewhat less attractive than learning about the exciting possibilities of power healing! However, the story of what happened to the prophet's widow in 2 Kings 4:1–7 offers a stimulus to us. In her plight, she had come to Elisha, to cry out to him for help. Her husband had revered the Lord. Yet he was now dead, and she was left with no more resources to provide for her family. The creditor was about to come to take her two boys as his slaves, and all she had left was a little oil. Elisha told her to go round to all her neighbours for empty jars. He told her not to ask just for a few. Then she was to start pouring the small amount of oil she had into all the jars, and as each was filled, to put it to one side. This she did, one at a time, and the oil kept flowing. Only when there was no other jar left did the oil stop flowing.

The story encourages us to believe that God will keep pouring out the oil of His teaching to us, providing we continue to keep putting out the jars to catch it. If we will only put out the jars that catch the oil of power healing and pastoral healing, that is all we will have. However, if we put out the jars of paschal healing as well, he will continue to give new oil. There will be just as much oil for healing as we are willing to put ourselves in a position to collect.

Moving faith

The toughness of the questions in healing ministry may suggest it has got stuck. Our reaction may be like that of Moses who, when the people of Israel were in crisis, stuck between the Egyptians and the sea said 'Do not be afraid. Stand firm and you will see the deliverance the Lord will bring you today. The Egyptians you see today you will never see again. The Lord will fight for you; you need only to be still.' (Exodus 14:13–14) Then, to quote from the Living Bible, God said to Moses 'Quit praying and get the people moving! Forward march!' It was a remarkable countermand to Moses' instructions. What was to follow was the most unprecedented in-break of God's power to deliver. First the pillar of cloud that had stood in front of the people of Israel moved to the rear so that the cloud brought darkness to one side and light to the other. Next, an eclipse took place which protected all those who were to be saved. Then as Moses stretched out his hand over the waters, they were divided and the people of Israel were enabled to cross over. Finally the entire army of pursuing Egyptians was drowned as the waters flowed back over them.

This is the way the Lord our Healer can move. Yet His mighty works of healing and deliverance still only happen if His people move when He says. It may look like faith to stand still in the face of the enemy and wait to see God do it all for us. It may look like faith to appear poised for the big take off. But until faith is exercised to press on towards the goal, we and the society in which we live are unlikely to see God's healing power break in as is so desperately needed.

It is probable that the next few years will be a watershed for the spiritual direction of many nations. For our part it may not be that God is saying to us at this time as He did to Moses 'Quit praying'. It could well be however that God is saying 'Get the people moving'.

Notes

Chapter 1

1 Peter Jennings, *Renewal*, February 1987, p10.
2 Jennifer Rees-Larcombe, *Unexpected Healing* (London, Hodder and Stoughton), p171.
3 See Paul Thigpen, *Alpha*, January 1993, p20.

Chapter 3

1 W.H. Vanstone, *The Stature of Waiting* (London, Darton, Longman and Todd 1982) p17f.
2 Henri J.M. Nouwen, *The Wounded Healer* (Image) p88.
3 Susan James, *Healed Within* (London, Hodder and Stoughton 1991).

Chapter 4

1 John Wimber, *Power Evangelism* (London, Hodder and Stoughton 1985) p26.

Chapter 5

1 David Watson, *Fear No Evil* (London, Hodder and Stoughton 1984) pp 137–8.
2 John and Paula Sandford, *Restoring the Christian Family* (Tulsa, Oklahoma, Victory House, 1979) p 142.

Chapter 7

1 Kenneth Copeland, *Healed, to be or not to be?* (Fort Worth, Texas, Kenneth Copeland Ministries Inc 1979) p 9.

2 Ibid., p13.
3 Ibid., p22.
4 Dan McConnell, *The Promise of Health and Wealth* (London, Hodder and Stoughton 1990) pp165, 169, 187.
5 Ibid., pp184, 185.
6 John and Paula Sandford, *Healing the Wounded Spirit* (Tulsa, Oklahoma, Victory, 1985) p 294.
7 Ibid., p166.
8 John Osteen, *There is a Miracle In Your Mouth* (John Osteen Publications) p27.
9 Julie Sheldon, *Dancer Off Her Feet* (London, Hodder and Stoughton, 1991), afterword.
10 David Watson, *Fear No Evil* (London Hodder and Stoughton, 1984) p107.
11 Adrian Chatfield, *Anglicans For Renewal*, Volume 44, spring 91.

Chapter 8

1 Douglas McBain, *Anglicans For Renewal*, winter 88/89, No. 35, p12.
2 Nigel Wright, *Renewal*, March 1989, p12.
3 John Wimber, *Power Healing* (London, Hodder and Stoughton, 1986) pp 171–2.

Chapter 9

1 Nigel Wright, *The Fair Face of Evil* (London, Marshall Pickering, 1989) p 41.
2 Billy Graham, *Angels: God's Secret Agents* (London, Hodder and Stoughton, 1976).
3 Francis Schaeffer, *The Great Evangelical Disaster* (Westchester, Illinois, Crossway, 1984) p115.
4 C.S. Lewis, *The Screwtape Letters* (London, Fount 1978) p.9.

Chapter 10

1 Richard Foster, *Money, Sex & Power* (London, Hodder and Stoughton, 1985). p. 13.
2 Luke T. Johnson, *Sharing Possessions*. (London, SCM, 1986) p49.
3 John & Paula Sandford, *op. cit.*, p344.
4 Ibid., p364.

Chapter 11

1 Anne Field OSB, *New Life* (London & Oxford, Mowbray 1978) p 189.
2 Dietrich Bonhoeffer, *The Cost of Discipleship* (London, SCM Press, 1950) p77.

Chapter 13

1 Mark Stibbe, *Anglicans For Renewal*, Volume 49, summer 92.
2 *Church of England Newspaper*, 27th March, 1992.
3 Chris Sugden, *Social Gospel or No Gospel?* (Bramcote, Notts, Grove Booklets, 1977) p9.
4 Richard Lovelace, *Dynamics of Spiritual Life* (Exeter, Paternoster Press 1979) pp387–8.
5 David Sheppard, *Built as a City* (London, Hodder and Stoughton 1974) p355.
6 Ray Bakke, International Urban Associates newsletter, summer 1992.

Chapter 14

1 Stephen Pile, *The Book of Heroic Failures* (London, Penguin Books, 1980) p17.

Chapter 15

1 C.S. Lewis *The Problem of Pain* (London & Glasgow, Collins Fontana, 1940) p49.
2 Tom Smail, *The Forgotten Father* (London, Hodder and Stoughton, 1980) p39.

Chapter 16

1 John Drane, *What is the New Age Saying to the Church* (Marshall Pickering, 1991), p18.

Chapter 17

1 Peter Brierley, *Vision Building* (London, Hodder and Stoughton, 1989) p26.